THE LOCKHEED F-117 *STEALTH* FIGHTER STORY

F-117A, 84-0828, following landing at Nellis AFB, Nevada on April 21, 1990, and immediately prior to being placed on public display for the first time in its history. Aircraft was specially painted for the occasion, with 37th TFW markings in off-white and gray visible on its vertical-tail surfaces. TAC/unit badges were seen on intake cheeks.

CREDITS:

This booklet is the end product of contributions and efforts made on behalf of the author and Aerofax, Inc. by the following individuals: John Andrews of Testor Corp., Capt. Kevin Baggetti, Michael Binder, Kearney Bothwell of Hughes, Tom Copeland, Greg Fieser, Rene' Francillon, Charles Fleming, Jim Goodall, Kelly Green, Lt. Eric Holman, E.S. "Mule" Holmberg of Hughes, Bob Johnson of Revell Models, John Kerr, Tony Landis, Capt. Greg Meland, Steven Miller of the 37th TFW, Scott Newman, Dick Pawloski, Chris Pocock, Ralph Poznecki, Ben Rich of Lockheed, Mick Roth, Robert Salvucci of GE Aircraft Engines, Bobby Shelton of the 37th TFW, Eva Smoke, Richard Stadler of Lockheed, Jim Stevenson, Bill Sweetman, Katsuhiko Tokunaga, Deborah Vito of Schubert & Company, Barbara Wasson, and Dwight Weber of General Electric.

AUTHOR'S COMMENTS:

This booklet has been assembled with only one purpose in mind. . . . to provide the many curious among us with detailed photographic insight into one of the most interesting flying machines of the past several decades—Lockheed's unique F-117 *Stealth* Fighter. The timing is purposefully close on the heels of the Department of Defense's long-delayed, but finally consummated decision, during early 1990, to release, within the constraints of security, as much information as possible concerning the F-117 and its mission objectives. Though much remains to be said about this aircraft, and considerably more will be released or leaked during the months and years ahead, this booklet represents a comprehensive summary to date, with considerable previously unpublished information and photography.

COUNTERING RADAR:

It is, of course, the military applications of radar that concern us in this book. Because of radar's extreme importance in locating targets for destruction, extraordinary emphasis has been placed on its development and utilization as well as devices capable of overcoming or countering its capabilities. The latter, in effect, is what the F-117 is all about. Its design has been optimized to create the smallest radar target possible. Coupled with other stealth characteristics described later, it is a second-generation attempt to develop an aircraft that is virtually impossible to track by radar in a combat scenario.

Basically, radar countering techniques (generally referred to as electronic countermeasures or ECM) which now are readily found on virtually all operational combat aircraft and also are applicable to other military hardware as well, can be divided into two broad but basic categories—passive and active. The former involves the utilization of the physical characteristics of the aircraft to mask, within limits, its actual visibility, radar cross-section, active emissions (electronic, infrared, and otherwise), and any other aspect that would reveal its presence to an enemy; and the latter involves the use of systems that actively jam, deceive, or in any other way physically inhibit the enemy's ability to locate and destroy its target via electronic means. When combined, the two disciplines usually are referred to as defensive electronic counter-measures (DECM).

Granted that the objective is to interfere with an enemy's air defense system by inhibiting its sensors, there are basically three options:

1. Radiate active signals optimized to interfere with the enemy's radar.

2. Change the electrical properties of the medium through which the radar's energy is being transmitted (usually the atmosphere).

3. Change the reflective properties of the aircraft itself.

The first of these encompasses most jamming and deception systems; the second includes devices such as chaff and absorbing aerosols; and the last includes technologies involving the basic design of the actual vehicle, RAM, and various types of echo distortion systems such as corner reflectors. A description of each follows:

1. Jammers can work in two ways—either by relying on brute force to overwhelm the hostile radar, or by confusing its accuracy. Some dual mode systems can do both. Types include:

(a) Noise jammers take the easy way out and

F-117A, 84-0828, is seen with auxiliary intake doors in full-open position. Landing gear stance is wide, making the aircraft very stable during landing and taxi. Noteworthy is generally flat fuselage undersurface.

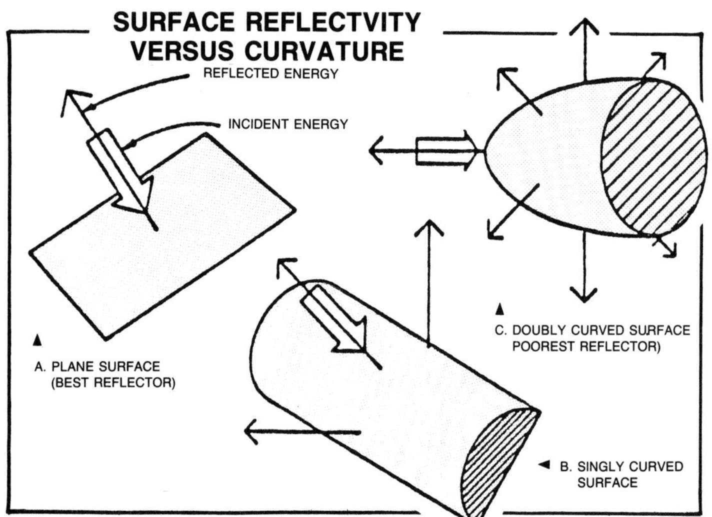

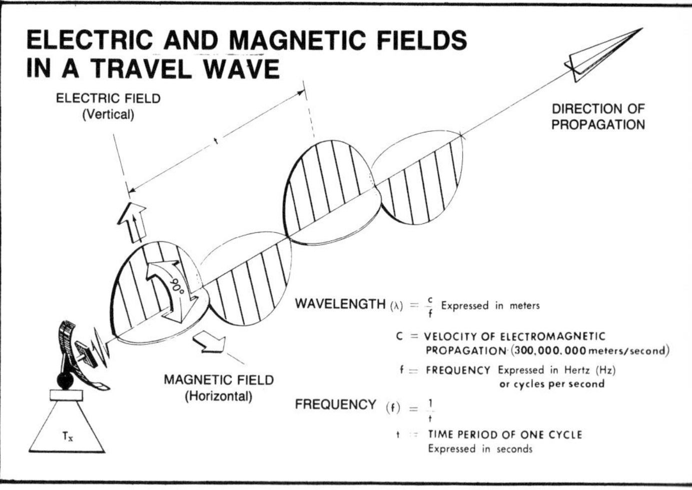

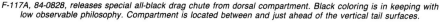

Jay Miller/Aerofax, Inc.

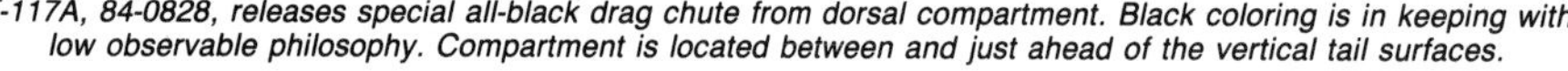
F-117A, 84-0828, releases special all-black drag chute from dorsal compartment. Black coloring is in keeping with low observable philosophy. Compartment is located between and just ahead of the vertical tail surfaces.

MAGNETRON

RESONANT CAVITIES
CATHODE
ANODE
ELECTRONS SPIRALING OUT IN CYCLOIDAL PATH
OUTPUT PROBE

attempt to drown the radar return from the target in an ocean of noise. Noise jamming has many advantages. Relatively few electronic intelligence data are required, and the ECM device will affect anything operating on the frequencies being jammed. The design techniques are simple since the ECM is merely out-shouting the hostile radar. Unfortunately some of the methods for countering noise jammers are equally as simple. The most obvious is to use frequency diversity (or "hopping") and to have a number of different radar frequencies on which to transmit.

(b) Spot noise jamming is the easiest method. A noise-modulated transmitter is set to operate on the frequency of the hostile emitter. This can be countered by enemy equipment fitted with a choice of operating frequencies.

(c) Swept-spot noise jammers continuously scan a range of operating frequencies, interfering with each in turn. As long as all operating frequencies are covered, the threat radar will be regularly disrupted.

(d) Barrage jammers are much simpler, radiating noise over the entire range of frequencies being covered, but for the same effect they need to be more powerful than spot jammers. Such equipment tends to be heavier than spot jammers, as well, but this is offset partially by the need for the latter to carry set-on receivers.

(e) Deception jammers are more complex than the noise generators described above and are based largely on the repeater principle, receiving the hostile signal then re-transmitting it in modified or delayed form (in such a way that the radar thinks it is seeing an echo from another aircraft with a different position or velocity). Surveillance radars build up a picture of the surrounding airspace but tracking radars must concentrate on a single target. This normally is done by a process known as gating. Once a target has been selected, a tracking radar does not listen continuously between output pulses from the target echo but only at around the time when the echo is expected. It thus is not confused by other targets nearer or further away from its antenna. As the target increases or decreases in range, the gate is moved accordingly. The interval of time between the radar output pulse being transmitted and the gated reply being received is used to measure target range. The gate effectively straddles the return signal within the radar receiver circuitry and is "smart" enough to move in time with the return. Signals outside the gate are simply ignored. Typical deception techniques utilized by these jammers include range-gate pull off, velocity track breaking, inverse amplitude modulation, inverse gain jamming, false target generation, buddy mode (using two aircraft), and cross eye (similar to buddy mode, but utilizing one aircraft with widely separated jamming system antennas).

2. There are basically two ways to change the electrical properties of the medium through which the radar's energy is being transmitted. The most common is via the use of small metallic strips called chaff (during World War II, chaff was referred to as "window") which work by affecting the propogation characteristics of the atmosphere, and the least common is through the very rare use of aerosols which contain metallic particulates.

Chaff operates against radar by creating and/or concealing targets, thereby creating confusion and delay. Chaff is used to assist aircraft in penetrating a radar network undetected and unidentified by creating a multitude of misleading targets or a large area of solid radar returns to confuse and mislead radar operators. Furthermore, even though the radar may locate the target, the addition of chaff induces errors in tracking radars and may disrupt tracking entirely. Chaff tends to saturate the capability of a radar and to create doubts, confusion, and hesitation among ground radar operators.

When first utilized during WWII against axis radar systems, chaff consisted of thin strips of aluminum foil with a length that was approximately half the wavelength of the radar being countered (today it is known that multiples of one-half the wavelength of the radar signal are suitable; this maximizes the sympathetic electrical resonance effect). The strips were purposefully made thin and light to enhance their ability to float in the atmosphere. Contemporary chaff is generally made of glass or plastic fiber material with a thin metallic film deposited on its surface. The lower density of these base materials enhances "float" characteristics.

Chaff is dispensed in bundles or by machines that can provide strips of varying length in response to the immediate radar threat. For use against low-frequency radars (50 to 100 MHz), lengths of 5 to 10 ft. are common; lower frequency systems, such as those operated by the Germans during World War II, sometimes required chaff strips with lengths of 100 ft. or more.

3. By changing the reflective properties of the aircraft itself, the aircraft's radar cross-section can be modified to a startlingly great degree. It is, in fact, this specific technology that is the essence of the Lockheed F-117's passive defensive system.

Work on materials that absorb, rather than reflect electromagnetic energy first was undertaken successfully by the Germans during World War II. The ability of allied aircraft-borne ASV (air-

Drag chute of F-117A, 84-0828, in fully inflated condition. Noteworthy in this view are the taxi lights. There is a single light attached to each gear strut. Triple-redundancy is the end product of the heavy emphasis being placed on operating the aircraft in total darkness.

to-surface-vessel) radar systems to pick up German submarine snorkels had proven a major frustration, and as a result, a rubberized radar absorbent material (RAM) was developed under a program referred to as *Schornfeinsteger* (Chimneysweep). This proved a modestly effective method of lowering the radar return from the snorkels, but it was far from foolproof—good radar operators often still could find the recharging submarines without significant difficulty.

Regardless, German RAM technology also was applied to other hardware including their aircraft. The most notable of the latter was the stunningly attractive Horten Ho IX. This tailless twin-jet fighter project, perhaps the most advanced in the world at the time of its debut during 1944, was of primarily wood construction (with steel tube framing). Abbreviated test flights were conducted during January of 1945, and were followed by an order for twenty production samples under the designation Gotha Go 229.

Unknown to all but a few, the Gotha variant of the Ho IX also was to become the first viable aircraft designed from the start to incorporate RAM. Though the three Horton Ho IX prototypes (one of which was an unpowered glider) had been built without it, the projected production aircraft would have utilized a wood-laminate skin consisting of two thin plastic-impregnated plywood sheets and a core material made of a sawdust, charcoal, and glue matrix. The latter, optimized to absorb radio energy with minimal return, was crude, but when coupled with the general construction materials of the rest of the aircraft, nevertheless contributed to what almost certainly would have been a very low radar cross section (RCS—i.e., the target's reflectivity in total).

Digressing for a moment, it should be noted that four basic factors determine the amount of reflected energy a radar will receive from a target during any one period of time that the antenna beam is trained on it: (1) the average power—rate of flow of energy—of the radio waves radiated in the target's direction; (2) the fraction of the wave's power which is intercepted by the target and scattered back in the radar's direction; (3) the fraction of that power which is captured by the radar antenna; and (4) the length of time the antenna beam is trained on the target.

Customarily, a target's geometric cross-sectional area, reflectivity, and directivity (the ratio of the power scattered back in the radar's direction to the power that would have been backscattered had the scattering been uniform in all directions—i.e., isotropically) are lumped together in what is called radar cross section (RCS). For computational purposes, this is represented by the Greek letter sigma, and is usually expressed in terms of square meters of area. The power density of the waves reflected back in the radar's direction, then, can be found by multiplying the power density of the transmitted waves when they reach the target by the target's RCS. Since the directivity of a target can be quite high, for some target aspects the RCS may be many times the geometric cross sectional area (the F-15, for instance, has an actual area of approximately 25 sq. meters when viewed from the side; its RCS, however, when viewed from the same aspect, is probably closer to 400 sq. meters; additional aircraft for comparison include the Boeing B-52 with an equivalent RCS of 1,076 sq. ft., the Rockwell B-1A with an RCS of 108 sq. ft., and the Rockwell B-1B, with an RCS of 11 sq. ft.). For others, the reverse may be true.

Regardless, the further away from the radar a target is, the lower the strength of the return echo. Assuming an arbitrary strength of 1 at 1 mile, echoes from a standard target at 50 mile range, for instance, are only 0.00000016 times as strong.

Though work on RAM and lowering RCS continued in many parts of the world during the closing stages of the war, its priority effectively remained low. During 1944, scientists at the prestigious Massachusetts Institute of Technology Radiation Laboratory created a ship-optimized RAM-type product referred to as "Halpern anti-radar paint" (HARP) with iron particulates suspended in a neoprene rubber base, but this saw little use and eventually was discarded. Additionally, and perhaps more importantly, an Air Force-sponsored research project of approximately the same era resulted in the development of a paint referred to as MX-410, which also was a rubber matrix, though differing in having disc-shaped aluminum flakes in place of HARP's iron particulates.

With the post-1950s profligation of radar systems around the world, and an ever-increasing surface-to-air missile barrier rising in what then was considered to be the main U.S. threat—the Soviet Union—interest in RCS and RAM technology began to resurface, though only as a secondary effort behind conventional electronic countermeasures and only at the most highly classified levels of government. In fact, the first aircraft created from scratch with RCS and RAM as integral elements of its design, Lockheed's A-12 high-speed, high-altitude reconnaissance aircraft, was a product of a Central Intelligence Agency requirement rather than that of any of the three major military services.

Work on the A-12 had been initiated during 1959, taking into consideration for the first time

Jay Miller/Aerofax, Inc.

F-117A, 80-0790, begins gear retraction sequence for go-around. All three landing gear retract forward into respective wells. During pass, aircraft sounded like virtually any other jet, though somewhat muted.

Jay Miller/Aerofax, Inc.

Landing roll-out for F-117A, 84-0828. Drag chute was released for ground crew pick-up moments later. Open drag chute compartment doors are visible just ahead of vertical tail surfaces. Visible are still-extended antennas.

the fact that resonance effects on straight portions of reflecting skin materials greater than a half-wavelength in dimension will radiate perpendicularly to the surface when illuminated by radar. It was discovered, however, that if the same surface was curved, the resonance effect would decrease by a mathematically computable ratio and the reflected energy would be distributed in several different directions. Thus curved surfaces returned considerably less energy to a radar receiver than flat.

With this in mind, Lockheed embarked on what was, to all intents and purposes, the first successful RCS-lowering blended fuselage design that combined aerodynamics with the exigencies of diminishing the aircraft's radar return. Chines and wings were successfully blended with the A-12's two engine nacelles and a long, tubular fuselage to create the first Mach 3 cruise-capable aircraft in history. Though 102 ft. long and with a wingspan of 55 ft. 7 in., its total RCS was only 22 sq. in.

Blending of components in the A-12, however, was not the end of Lockheed's initial approach to what became known as "stealth" technology. In addition, the company integrated into the aircraft's basic design RAM-type structural elements called corner reflectors. These devices, which were integral with the wing and fuselage chine leading edge surfaces (thus giving the leading edge surface paneling a saw-tooth or dog-tooth look) were formed from three intersecting, mutually perpendicular metal (titanium) sheets. When installed, they reflected energy like any other metal surface, but the difference was that their triangular configuration created a very effective energy trap. In the A-12, for additional attenuation, a pyroceramic insert matrixed with its own attenuators was used as a filler to give the wing leading edge continuity, aerodynamic integrity, and the ability to withstand the rigors of cruising flight at three times the speed of sound.

RAM, it was discovered, could be manufactured from a wide variety of materials with each providing a unique or energy-specific capability. Concerning the latter, RAM was found to be most efficient when utilized in thicknesses that were dimensionally a quarter of the specific wavelength being attenuated and also permeable to electromagnetic energy. When applied in layers, energy reflected repeatedly between them was rapidly dissipated and returns were minimized.

Unfortunately, first-generation RAMs came with a hefty price. In many instances, they were applied to external parts of the aircraft and were not load-bearing, and this resulted in both aerodynamic and weight penalties. With the sole exception of the then-highly-classified A-12 (and, it should be mentioned, one of its never-to-be-built competitors, General Dynamics' highly-classified *Kingfish* project; the latter was to have been manufactured almost entirely of pyroceram; it would have been capable of Mach 6.25 at an altitude of 125,000 ft.), they were rarely considered as integral elements of the airframe.

Topping off the attention to lowering the A-12's RCS was a covering of radar absorbent paint (initially this was applied to the most reflective elements, only; later, the entire aircraft was painted). Basically a matrix consisting of a suspension base (epoxy) and ferrite (iron) particulates, it worked on the same fundamental principles of other RAMs in that the molecular structure was optimized to absorb (in the form of "free electron" activity converted to heat) as much of the incoming radar energy as possible. Though only modestly effective (much of the radar's energy was still reflected), when combined with other design techniques and the more aggresive forms of structural RAM, it provided a rather large payoff in lowering the aircraft's total RCS.

Little information has entered the public domain concerning RAMs and their physical characteristics. The following list, however, was provided by Plessey Microwave of England and gives some insight into this relatively esoteric subject:

A-1 Netting—A broadband, moderate-performance, low-cost material covering 4 GHz up to 94 to 100 GHz. Main applications are reducing RCS outside installations such as hardened aircraft shelter doors. For it to be utilized in harsh environments, it must be encapsulated in a PVC or plastic envelope. It has numerous applications.

Salisbury Screen—If material is needed to work down at a lower than normal operational frequency, it can be utilized in this form, which consists of a back-reflecting mechanism such as a wire mesh, metallic mesh, sheet material, or even a garden fence. There is a dielectric airspace between the absorber on the front surface and the rear surface, with the distance calculated depending on the operating frequency required. At 1 GHz its performance is increased from about 12 or 15 dB to about 20 dB. There is a third harmonic performance from the base frequency (1GHz) at 3 GHz, 5 GHz, 7GHz, and so on.

IRAM—The base material for this is horsehair packing (exactly the same as commonly available for other, more domestic requirements). Its main use is to absorb stray energy and sidelobes from communication antennas. It is inexpensive, but it has moderate performance in the 15 dB range, having a frequency excursion of about 4 GHz up to 16 GHz. It is available in sheets with sizes of 8 ft. by 2 ft.

LA O (La Nought)—A high-performance material consisting of reticulated polyurethane foam treated with carbon emulsions. Its performance (frequency range) is dependent upon the thickness required. At 6mm, it would have a high-performance broadband from approximately 20 GHz up to 100 GHz; in 12mm thickness the bottom frequency would improve with coverage of from 4 GHz to in excess of 50 GHz; in the 2 in. thick version a bottom operating frequency of 1 to 1.5 GHz would be possible, but reasonable performance would occur in the 30 to 50 GHz range. This product has many applications ranging from antennas to missile nosecones. If LA O is "foamed through" with a low-loss dielectric foam, its characteristic is changed into a flexible sheet which is very rigid with a high mechanical strength. In this form, it can be fabricated or molded into virtually any shape desired. Where weight is a significant problem, and flexibility of the product is required, LA O can be machined into whatever is required.

ADRAM (Advanced Dielectric Radar Absorbent Material)—The base material is polyurethane, but it is loaded with a dielectric (plastic or insulating) material. Performance is similar to that of the narrow-band materials. It has a high angle-of-incidence property (it can operate at angles-of-incidence in excess of 120° included angle) whereas the narrow-band materials operate at + or - 50°. The need for high angle-of-incidence performance is to get multi-bounce, multi-path reflections of high-energy, whereas the single-tuned frequencies operate at (basically) 90° to the incoming signal (the original single-frequency materials were used on various aircraft projects during the 1950s, but weight problems precluded widespread use).

Sheet Materials—Using rubbers, nitriles, silicones, and polyurethanes as bases, it is possible to load them with various magnetically-loaded products such as ferrous materials, carbons, and

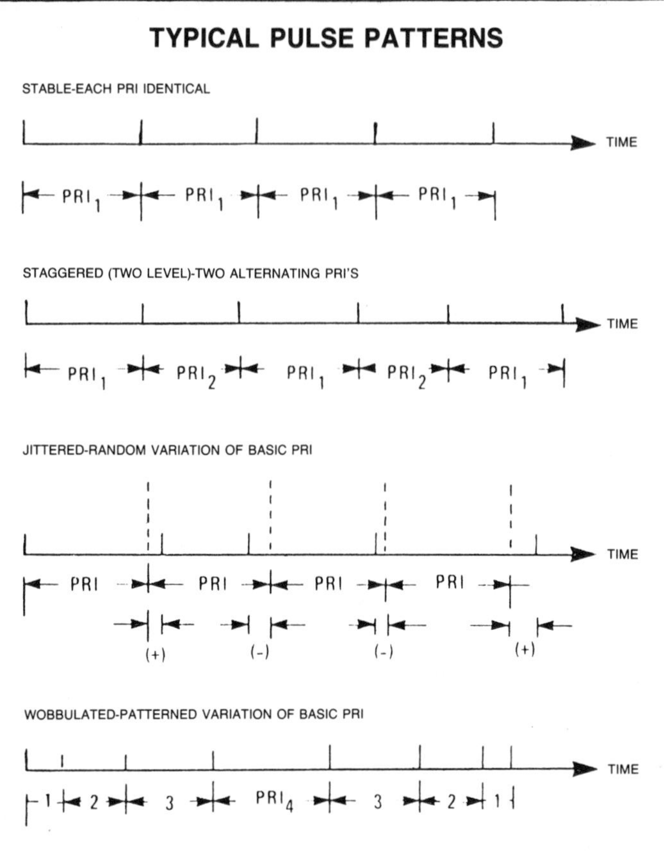

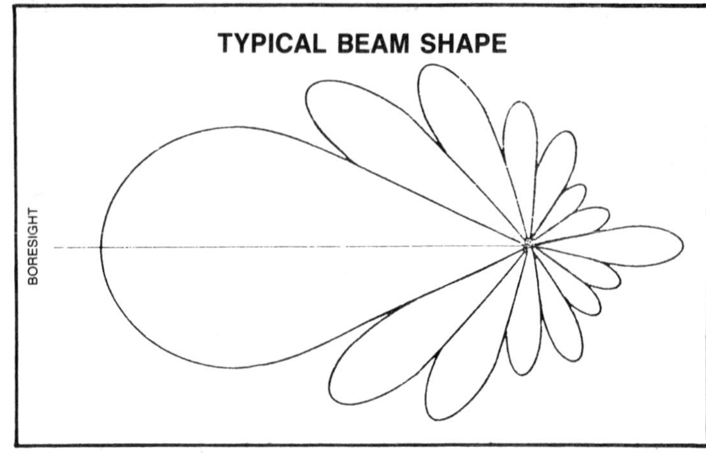

Jay Miller/Aerofax, Inc.

F-117A, 84-0828, was given special "high visibilty" markings for airshow circuit. Aircraft is expected to appear at up to two shows per month during 1989-1990.

high-performance dielectrics. These are high-performance narrow-band items which can be manufactured in mouldings which bond two materials together (for example, one tuned to S-band and one tuned to X-band). The performance is in excess of 25 dB at the chosen operating frequencies. Application is limited because of weight.

Additionally, during the early 1960s, it is known that Lockheed developed and flight tested a first-generation RAM product utilizing a Salisbury Screen and a rubberized coating called Echosorb. This matrix was tested extensively by the company as a U-2 undersurface coating before being shelved due to general ineffectivity and maintenance difficulties. Still more recently, the Japanese company, TDK, revealed that it sells a commercial RAM consisting of two layers of ferrites with different characteristics that can be utilized to absorb microwaves for commercial purposes (such as on tall buildings to absorb television signals or correct problems with television ghosting).

The other passive elements involved in masking an aircraft's presence lie in controlling its infrared (IR) signatures, its accoustical signature, and its exhaust emissions. Infrared radiation is electromagnetic radiation with a dual quality. The principal feature distinguishing IR from radar energy is its position in the electromagnetic spectrum. The frequency of IR radiation extends from approximately one million to five-hundred million megaHertz. In the frequency spectrum, IR falls between the upper limit of microwaves and the lower limit of light. Because of this location, it exhibits some of the characteristics of microwaves and some of the characteristics of light waves. IR, interestingly, can be transmitted through materials opaque to visible light, and IR also can be optically focused by lenses and mirrors. Any material whose temperature is above absolute zero (zero degrees on the Kelvin temperature scale; or -273 degrees centigrade) generates IR radiation. If the material is heated, not only does the kinetic energy of the molecules increase, but also the electrons in each atom are raised to a higher energy level. As the material cools, it gives up this energy and the electrons fall back to their original energy level. This energy level change causes electromagnetic radiations, some of which fall into the IR wavelength range. Because IR is produced by warm materials and because temperature dictates the characteristics of the radiation from these materials, IR energy is often erroneously referred to as "heat waves". IR is not heat, but depends on heat for generation.

The development of IR systems has been paralleled by a search for effective IR countermeasures (IRCM). IRCM can be either specifically designed equipment to affect target homing ability of an IR seeker, or it can be specific tactics designed to affect target discrimination ability. Importantly, through passive elements such as design, the detectability of a target such as an aircraft may be decreased by shielding the hot components of an engine from view or by reducing the engine operating temperature.

Efficient use of some IRCM requires warning of the presence of an IR threat. Since IR systems can attack without the use of a supporting radar search and track system for acquisition, airborne IR warning receivers have been developed to passively detect the presence of the attacker's exhaust plume. Airborne IR warning receivers are capable not only of detecting the presence of an airborne interceptor, but they also can detect the launch of an air-to-air missile. Once the IR homing missile has been launched, IR countermeasures can be employed.

One IR countermeasure is the introduction of smoke into the exhaust of the target aircraft's jet engine(s) to diffuse engine-generated IR radiation.

Another IRCM is the flare. Flares are designed to produce a greater source of IR radiation than the target aircraft's jet engines. The flare is ejected from the aircraft, and as it falls away, the IR homing missile will track the flare and not the original target aircraft. The major disadvantage of flares is that only a limited number can be carried.

Another IRCM is the use of a powerful IR source, such as a lamp, that can be installed in the tail of an aircraft. By blinking the lamp on and off at a predetermined rate, an IR homing missile can be deceived in much the same way that a radar can be angle-deceived. The advantage of this IRCM type is that the supply of countermeasures does not run out.

Tactical maneuvering is another form of IRCM. The aircraft may be able to evade the IR seeker's field of view, or it may maneuver so as to place the missile's IR detector view into the sun. If the latter maneuver is successful, the missile will not be able to separate the target from background radiation. Maneuvering into a cloud bank where the water droplets and dust particles will absorb and scatter the aircraft IR radiation is another IRCM.

Perhaps the penultimate example of IRCM is represented in the F-117A. Lockheed engineers went to great lengths to ensure that the infrared signature of this aircraft was kept to an absolute minimum. Exhaust gases are mixed with relatively cool ambient air in a plenum just aft of the engine compartment. The cooling air arrives via ducting that brings it from slots located in front of and below the intakes. Once mixed, the exhaust then is passed through a horizontal slot-type nozzle assembly that is some six feet wide and approximately six inches deep. This slot is divided into twelve separate ports which serve to channel the exhaust gases into an extended lower lip which is actually the flattened empennage of the aircraft. There the exhaust gases are again mixed rapidly with ambient air. By the time they enter the aircraft slipstream, temperature levels have been lowered significantly and the exhaust plume presents a minimal infrared target.

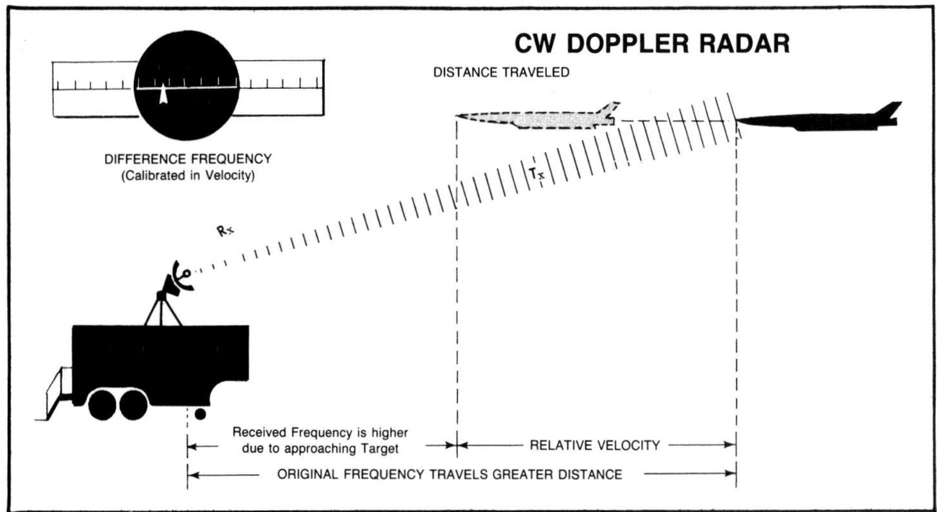

DOPPLER SHIFT FOR DIFFERENT RELATIVE VELOCITIES

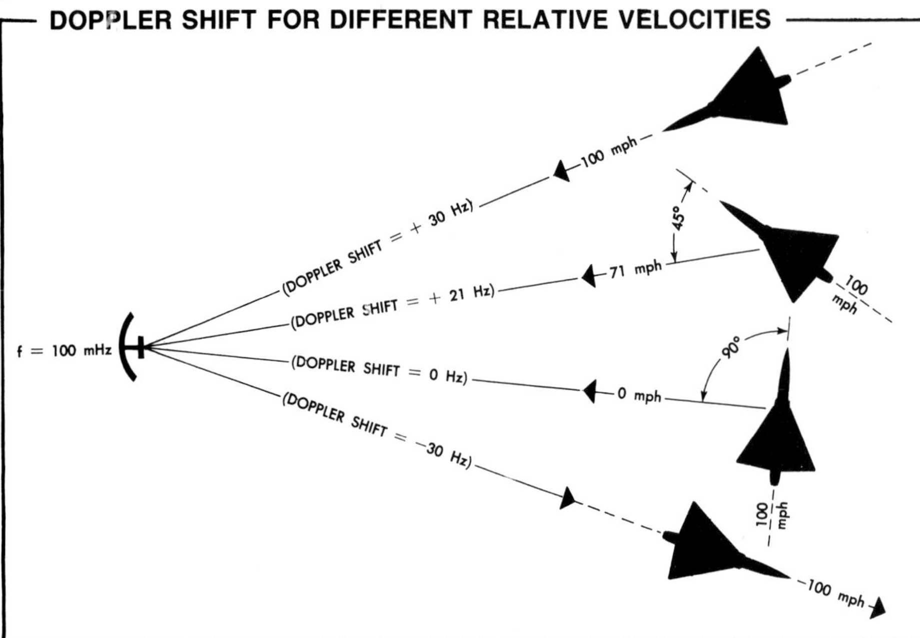

F-117:

On August 22, 1980, the following statement by then-Secretary of Defense Harold Brown (under President Jimmy Carter) was released to the public:

"I am announcing today a major technological advance of great military significance.

"This so-called 'stealth' technology enables the United States to build manned and unmanned aircraft that cannot be successfully intercepted with existing air defense systems. We have demonstrated to our satisfaction that the technology works.

"This achievement will be a formidable instrument of peace. It promises to add a unique dimension to our tactical forces and the deterrent strength of our strategic forces. At the same time it will provide us capabilities that are wholly consistent with our pursuit of verifiable arms control agreements, in particular, with the provisions of SALT II.

"For three years, we have successfully maintained the security of this program. This is because of the conscientious efforts of the relatively few people in the Executive Branch and the Legislative Branch who were briefed on the activity and of the contractors working on it.

"However, in the last few months, the circle of people knowledgeable about the program has widened, partly because of the increased size of the effort, and partly because of the debate underway in the Congress on new bomber proposals. Regrettably, there have been several leaks about the stealth program in the last few days in the press and television news coverage.

"In the face of these leaks, I believe that it is not appropriate or credible for us to deny the existence of this program. And it is now important to correct some of the leaked information that misrepresented the Administration's position on a new bomber program. The so-called stealth bomber was *not* a factor in our decision in 1977 to cancel the B-1; indeed, it was not yet in design.

"I am gratified that, as yet, none of the most sensitive and significant classified information about the characteristics of this program has been disclosed. An important objective of the announcement today is to make clear the kinds of information that we intend scrupulously to protect at the highest security level. Dr. Perry, my Under Secretary of Defense for Research and Engineering and a chief architect of this program will elaborate this point further.

"In sum, we have developed a new technology of extraordinary military significance. We are vigorously applying this technology to develop a number of military aircraft and these programs are showing very great promise.

"We can take tremendous pride in this latest achievement of American technology. It can play a major role in strengthening our strategic and tactical forces without in any way endangering any of our arms control initiatives. And it can contribute to the maintenance of peace by posing a new and significant offset to the Soviet Union's attempt to gain military ascendancy by weight of numbers.

"I would now like to ask Bill Perry to give you some additional details on our stealth program."

Under Secretary of Defense for Research and Engineering William Perry's comments were:

"World War II demonstrated the decisive role that air power can play in military operations. It also demonstrated the potential of radar as a primary means of detecting aircraft and directing fire against them. On balance, though, the advantage clearly was with the aircraft. Subsequent to World War II, defensive missiles—both ground-launched and air-launched—were developed and "married" with radar fire control systems. This substantially increased the effectiveness of air defense systems, shifting the balance against aircraft. For the last few decades we have been working on techniques to defeat such air defense systems. At present, our military aircraft make substantial use of electronic countermeasures (jamming) and flying low to place themselves in 'ground clutter', both of which degrade the effectiveness of air defense radars. By these means we have maintained the effectiveness of our military aircraft in the face of radar-directed defensive missiles.

"However, the Soviets continue to place very heavy emphasis on the development and deployment of air defense missiles in an attempt to offset the advantage we have in air power. They have built thousands of surface-to-air missile systems, they employ radars with high power and monopulse tracking circuits which are very difficult to jam, and in the last few years they have developed air-to-air missiles guided by 'look down' radars which are capable of tracking aircraft in 'ground clutter'.

"Because of these developments and because of the importance we attach to maintaining our air superiority, we have for years been developing what we call 'penetration' technology: the technology that degrades the effectiveness of radars and other sensors used by air defense systems. A particular emphasis has been on developing that technology which makes an aircraft 'invisible' (a figure of speech) to radar. In the early 1960s, we applied a particular version of this technology to some of our reconnaissance aircraft. In the mid-1970s we applied it to the cruise missiles then being developed (*Tomahawk* and ALCM). By the summer of 1977 it became clear that this technology could be considerably extended in its effectiveness and could be applied to a wide class of vehicles including manned aircraft. We concluded that it was possible to build aircraft so difficult to detect that they could not be successfully engaged by any existing air defense systems. Recognizing the great significance of such a development we took three related actions: first, we made roughly a ten-fold increase in our investment to advance this technology; second, we initiated a number of very high priority programs to apply this technology; and third, we gave the entire program extraordinary security protection, even to the point of classifying the very existence of such a program.

"Initially we were able to limit knowledge of the program to a very few Government officials in both the Executive and Legislative Branches and succeeded in maintaining complete secrecy about the program. However, as the program increased in size—currently the annual funding is 100 times greater than when we decided to accelerate the program in 1977—it became necessary to brief more people. The existence of a stealth program has now become public knowledge. But even as we acknowledge the existence of a stealth program, we will draw a new security line to protect that information about the program which could facilitate a Soviet countermeasures program. We will continue to protect at the highest security level information about:

a. the specific techniques which we employ to reduce detectability;

b. the degree of success of each of these techniques;

c. characteristics of specific vehicles being developed;

d. funds being applied to specific programs; and

e. schedules of specific programs.

"With those ground rules, I think you can see that I am extremely limited in what I can tell you about the program. I will say this. First, stealth technology does not involve a single technical approach, but rather a complex synthesis of many. Even if I were willing to describe it to you, I could not do it in a sentence or even a paragraph. Second, while we have made remarkable advances in the technology in the last three years, we have been building on excellent work done in our defense technology program over the last two decades. Third, this technology—theoretically at least—could be applied to any military vehicle which can be attacked by radar-directed fire. We are considering all such applications and are moving with some speed to develop those applications which are the most practical and which have the greatest military significance. Fourth, we have achieved excellent success on the program, including flight tests of a number of different vehicles."

Jay Miller/Aerofax, Inc.

F-117A, 80-0790, taxies onto Nellis AFB ramp following landing. Particularly noteworthy are still-extended communications/navigation antennas visible on top of and under fuselage. Antennas were retracted moments later.

As Brown and Perry implied, work on stealth-optimized—or low-observable—aircraft had been on-going for a considerable period of time by the date of their 1980 announcement. Many companies, most notably the Lockheed-California operation's Burbank facility and their unique Advanced Development Projects ("Skunk Works") operation (where the U-2, A-12, F-12, SR-71, and D-21 aircraft were developed), had long since forged ahead with reduced radar signature projects of one kind or another, and several, including Lockheed, had resulted in flightworthy hardware.

Though Lockheed had long been a leader in the basic technology thrust behind the reduction of an aircraft's radar signature, they were not included in a 1973 list of five companies (all with recent fighter manufacturing experience) asked to submit design studies as part of a highly classified Defense Advanced Research Projects Agency (DARPA) flying prototype contract under the blanket codename of *Have Blue*. Lockheed nevertheless asked for, and was given, permission to participate and by the end of the competition, had won over General Dynamics (with their Model 100), Northrop, McDonnell Douglas, Grumman, and Boeing. Accordingly Lockheed during 1974 received an approximately $30-million contract to design, manufacture, and test fly three two-thirds-scale twin-engine (General Electric J85) testbed aircraft. At the same time, Boeing also received a contract—though for two low-observable prototypes, rather than three.

Lockheed's efforts, headed by ADP manager Ben Rich, centered on an approach to lowering RCS that placed heavy emphasis on two major techniques: the use of RAM, and the idea that energy reflected *away* from a radar's receiver is the same as energy that has been absorbed and/or dissipated. Accordingly, because there then were limits to a computer's ability to simulate the RCS of curved surfaces, their design approach began with the development of a computer base that would assimilate all available data on angular vectors for radar generated energy reflected from flat surfaces. Radar viewing, it then was determined, almost always occurred within a 30° angle above or below the horizontal plane of the aircraft in level flight. Thus, if an aircraft's exterior paneling could be made of flat, or faceted, reflective surfaces that were installed at angles greater than 30°, re-radiated radar energy would not be returned to the radar's receiver—particularly in a situation where the mission flight path of the aircraft could be kept within a pre-established set of attitude parameters.

Because the effectiveness of RAM tended to be limited to the frequency range for which it was optimized, the difficulty now became how to pick a RAM with the broadest coverage and yet stay within the aerodynamic and structural limits of the aircraft. Eventually, as a result of a computer-generated set of priorities (depending on exposure odds), six different kinds of RAM were chosen for flat panel application. Thus it was assumed that by combining RAM with what was being termed "unshared reflectivity angles", this approach would provide a considerably more effective, across-the-board radar-defeating technology.

Still another element became the integration of the flat surfaces into an aerodynamically suitable shell. It became apparent the aircraft would of necessity be subsonic (as supersonic performance simply would not be required for its mission, anyway), and this eased some of the basic requirements. However, mating the flat plate edges, which were the most reflective elements in the entire design, was nevertheless critical, as linearity was an extraordinarily important factor in the RCS figure and concommitantly in the aircraft's basic aerodynamics. Additionally, all aerodynamic surfaces, such as the wing and vertical tail leading edges, were to be straight lines, with no return-generating breaks. Sweep angles, like the flat-

With 37th TFW markings readily visible on vertical tail, F-117A, 84-0828, taxies-in to display position at Nellis AFB. Drag chute compartment doors are still open and TAC badge is readily visible on starboard intake cheek. Aircraft is considerably larger than it appears and in fact is comparable dimensionally to the McDonnell Douglas F-15 "Eagle".

With 416th squadron markings readily visible on vertical tail, F-117A, 80-0790, taxies-in to display position at Nellis AFB next to 84-0828. Blow-in doors are in full-open position at this point, as normal intake capture area is not sufficient for efficient engine operation during taxi.

plate panels, also prevented direct returns from head-on radar coverage.

By late 1975, even though there were then limits to RCS simulation capability, work with the company's Cray computer system had generated a suitable design profile and as a result, construction of the three prototype aircraft (which some sources claim were known as XSTs—"experimental, stealth, tactical") was initiated. Roll-out took place during early 1977, and by the middle of the year, two of the three had been delivered to the classified Groom Lake, Nevada flight test facility and flown for the first time. The third aircraft, which remained at Burbank, served as a structural test article and was purposefully destroyed.

The relatively short-duration flight test program quickly verified Lockheed's theories. The various radar test ranges around Groom Lake and the nearby Nellis AFB test range, some of which included captured samples of Soviet radar systems, found the small aircraft extremely difficult to locate and track, and if evasive tactical maneuvers were utilized, the aircraft were quite literally "invisible". RCS numbers of "hundredths of a square meter" were said to be applicable, and this proved sufficient to merit further strong support for a full-scale production version of the basic design.

Eventually, both flightworthy Lockheed prototypes were lost in accidents. The first, with company test pilot Bill Park at the controls, occurred during a flight on May 5, 1978 and was the result of a landing gear malfunction. Park ejected, but was seriously injured when his seat failed to separate for a clean parachute deployment. The second aircraft, with company test pilot Ken Dyson at the controls, was lost several months later when it was consumed by a fire attributed to a hydraulic system failure. Dyson egressed the aircraft without injury, but the fire proved uncontrollable and the aircraft was a total write-off.

During 1978, following an assessment of the prototype results, the Air Force moved ahead with a decision to develop a full-scale production version of the original Lockheed design under the program codename *Senior Trend*. By now, mission objectives had been generated and it thus had become possible for Lockheed to narrow its design focus. The attributes of the aircraft's low RCS were ideally suited for ground support missions, and as a result the production aircraft was to be designed around that very specific requirement.

The new aircraft was to be optimized to covertly penetrate dense threat environments and attack high value targets with pinpoint weapon accuracy. Heavy emphasis would be placed on making the aircraft totally autonomous, totally passive, and as elusive a target as technologically possible; it would not be dependent upon external communications of any kind in order to accomplish its mission. Heavy emphasis would be placed on maintaining an almost negligible RCS, lowering the infrared (IR) signature, reducing the noise (acoustical) signature, reducing visibility (via size and paint constraints), and reducing powerplant visible emissions (exhaust particulates and contrail generation).

Under Ben Rich, the Lockheed Aeronautical Systems Company's Advanced Development Projects office formally began work on the full-scale development (FSD) aircraft during December of 1978 after receiving production approval from then-President Jimmy Carter. Though Air Force requirements originally had limited acquisition to twenty aircraft, Congressional pressure calling for the creation of a full wing (two squadrons) later led to a total buy of 59. Lockheed's contract, interestingly, included warranties covering the aircraft's range, weapon delivery accuracy, and RCS.

Though manufacture of the aircraft initially proved difficult because of the precision required during assembly to meet the RCS requirements, 31 months after FSD was authorized, the prototype, on June 15, 1981 took to the air from Groom Lake for the first time. The first production aircraft (reportedly 80-0785) was flown on January 15, 1982, and was followed at Burbank by others at a rate of one aircraft every 8 to 10 weeks. In the interim the test program was accelerated and the flight envelope was expanded. Problems were encountered with many of the aircraft's unorthodox features but in general it was found easy to fly and maintain.

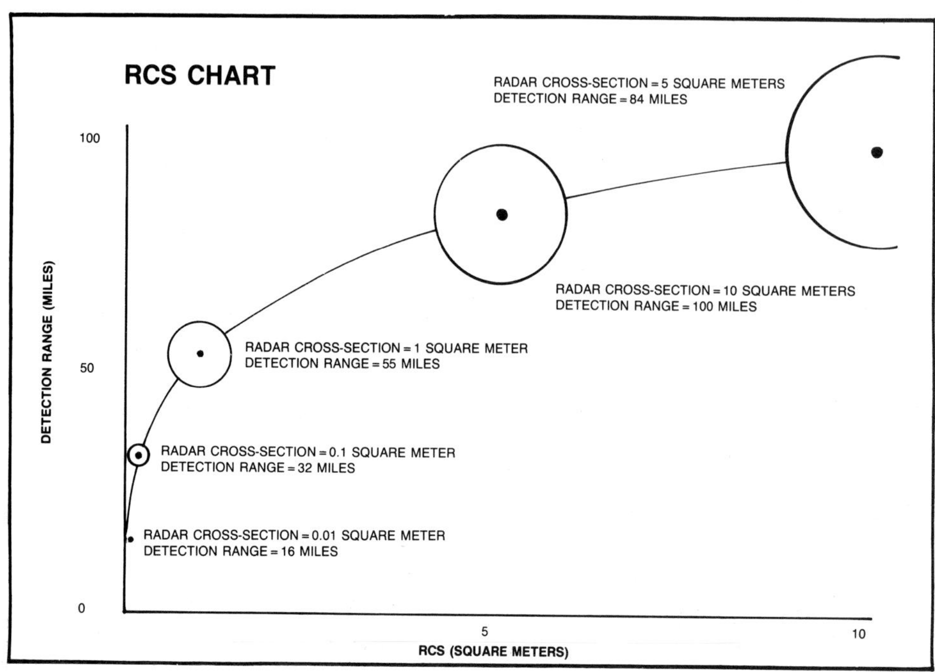

The advent of the new aircraft's development and flight test program, under the management of the Air Force's Aeronautical Systems Division, brought with it the added security requirement of communication without identification. Accordingly, similar to other exotic aircraft types flying in the southern Nevada area, an arbitrary radio call of "117" was assigned. This same radio call had been used by the enigmatic 4477th "Red Hats/Red Eagles" unit that often had flown expatriated MiGs in the area, but there was no relationship to the call and the formal F-19 designation then being considered by the Air Force. Apparently, use of the "117" radio call became commonplace and when Lockheed released its first flight manual ("dash one"), F-117A was the designation imprinted on the cover.

Additionally, though not officially acknowledged, the aircraft has acquired several nicknames and one semi-official moniker that seems to meet with just about everybody's liking. Pilot's and the press have, on occasion, referred to the aircraft as the *Wobbly Goblin* or *Bat Jet*, and there is some indication that the codename *Blue Maria* was utilized. However, the name that seems to be in favor, both formally and otherwise, is *Nighthawk*, and there is apparently strong indication that it will be officially designated as such following a more open integration into the Air Force inventory.

Flight testing of the F-117A was undertaken at both Groom Lake and a new facility at the old WWII-vintage Tonopah Test Range Airfield (elevation, 5,540 ft.) 140 miles northwest of Las Vegas (and Nellis AFB), Nevada and conveniently positioned between the Cactus and Kawich mountain ranges. Located near the old silver mining town of Tonopah and often referred to as TTR (Tonopah Test Range), it had undergone a major refurbishment following a 1981 Air Force decision to move all F-117 operational activity from Groom Lake (though all first flights, following truck delivery from Lockheed, continued to be conducted there).

Jay Miller/Aerofax, Inc.

F-117A 80-0790 (left), and 84-0828 (right) are seen shortly after their arrival at Nellis AFB on April 21, 1990. Ground crew is post-flight checking the aircraft prior to taxi into display area. Antennas were still extended.

Refurbishment, as part of the original Lockheed contract, included the construction of some 54 hangars, a general runway overhaul including a length increase from 10,000 to 12,500 ft., and accommodations for some 2,500 personnel.

Pilot recruitment for the program primarily was on a volunteer basis. Tours were for three years (this requirement is now being changed to two) and crews were not allowed to bring their families to Tonopah (instead, they were forced to find accommodations for them in nearby desert towns or in Las Vegas, proper—while commuting between home and base via contract transport aircraft—usually Key Airline). Minimum flight time required as pilot-in-command was 1,000 hours. Initial training took place in Vought A-7Ds (during 1989, concurrent with the formation of the 37th TFW, these were replaced by Northrop T-38As and AT-38As) during daylight flights, and this was followed by preliminary hops out to a radius of 200 miles from Tonopah in the F-117A at night. As proficiency increased, longer flights were undertaken, until the pilot was declared both proficient and combat ready. To date, the longest missions known to have been flown in the F-117 have lasted some 12 hours with inflight refueling. Present practice sortie rates result in pilots logging 15 to 20 hours per month in the F-117A and another 5 or 6 hours per month in the AT-38.

The first operational-standard production aircraft was turned over to the Tactical Air Command's 4450th Tactical Group during 1982, and on October 26, 1983, initial operational capability (IOC) was attained (with the 415th TFS—the 416th followed during January). The group initially was a direct reporting unit to the Tactical Air Command, Langley AFB, Virginia. During 1985, however, operational command was transferred to the Tactical Fighter Weapons Center, Nellis, AFB, Nevada. During October of 1989, it became the 37th Tactical Fighter Wing (under the operational command of the 12th Air Force, headquartered at Bergstrom AFB, Texas) comprised of the 415th and 416th Tactical Fighter Squadrons,

Jay Miller/Aerofax, Inc.

Extreme angularity of F-117A is readily apparent in this view of 84-0828. Sometimes referred to as a prism effect, the flat plating is optimized to minimize the direct return of radar energy. Elevons and flaperons sag once hydraulic pressure has bled. FLIR port, covered with screen-like material, is readily visible under forward windscreen transparency.

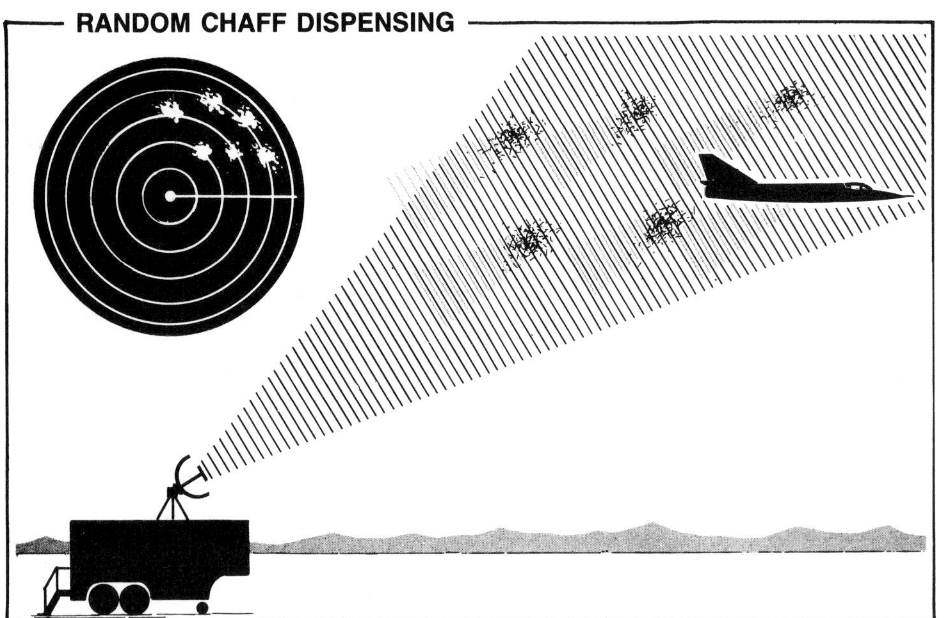

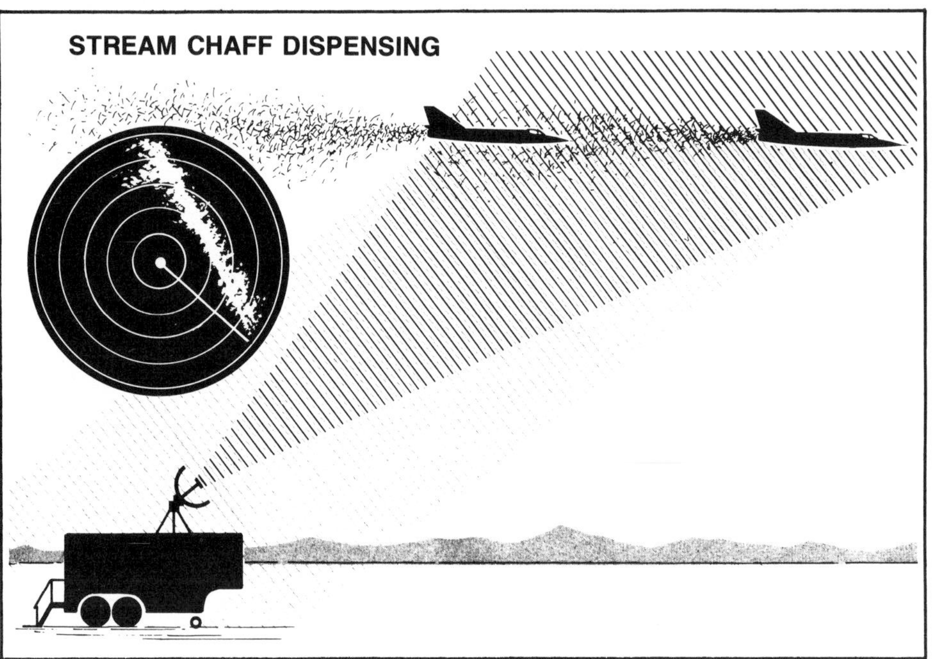

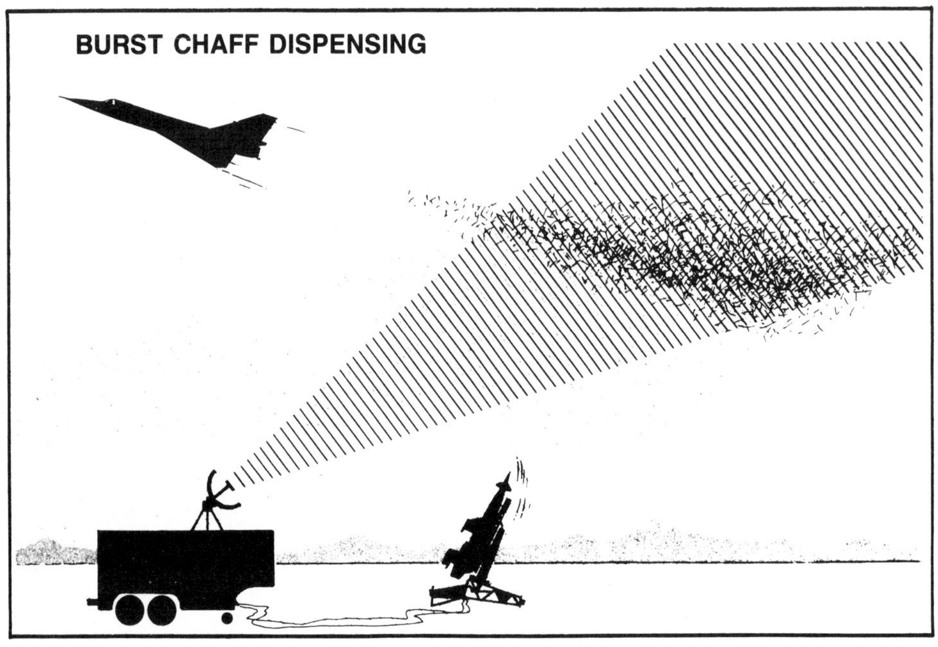

and the 417th Tactical Fighter Training Squadron. Present plans call for it to be moved from Tonopah to Holloman AFB, New Mexico during the spring of 1992. Holloman will lose the 479th Tactical Training Wing which operates 111 Northrop T-38A/AT-38B aircraft. Weather, traffic, and airspace availability have been cited as reasons for the move. However, accessibility to the White Sands Missile Range and McGregor, Oscura, Beak, and Talon ranges for training were important factors. Following the move, Tonopah will become a deployment site for Red Flag.

Prior to public acknowledgement of the aircraft by the Department of Defense during November of 1988, all information pertaining to its existence and activities was denied. All flight operations from Tonopah were conducted at night, and special precautions, such as keeping the aircraft hangar-bound until 30 minutes after sunset, and conducting ground operations in blacked-out conditions, were standard.

Because of these constraints, pilot workloads (which sometimes involved two flights a night) were considered inordinately high and there were problems. Complaints concerning spatial disorientation and fatigue were not uncommon, and at least two of three acknowledged accidents were thought to have been attributable to related difficulties. The first production aircraft crashed on June 21, 1982 during a test flight on the Nellis range (the Lockheed pilot survived). Later, two other aircraft crashed, these including 81-0792 on July 11, 1986 15 n. miles northeast of Bakersfield, California, and 83-0815 on October 14, 1987, on the Nellis range. In both of the latter accidents the Air Force pilots, Maj. Ross E. Mulhare and Maj. Michael C. Stewart, respectively, were killed.

On the plus side, the 37th TFW already has been recognized for its distinguished service and accomplishments. Top performance has earned it superior ratings during Operational Readiness Inspections. During 1988, the 4450th TG was awarded the TAC Commander's Maintenance Award in the Special Mission category. During 1989, the Air Force Association honored the F-117A program with its "Most Outstanding Service to National Defense in Manned Flight" award. Perhaps most significantly, during the same year, the prestigious Collier Trophy for "The Greatest Achievement in Aeronautics or Astronautics in America" was presented to "Ben R. Rich and the entire Lockheed/Air Force team for the production and deployment of the F-117A stealth aircraft which changes the entire concept of military aircraft design and combat deployment for the future"

Daylight proficiency was not ignored during this period and accommodating this were missions in Vought A-7Ds assigned to the 4450th. Tailcoded LV, these aircraft were standard *Corsair IIs* and, contrary to popular impression, were not specially modified in any way. On several occasions, the A-7Ds were spotted "out of country"—most notably in England. The A-7Ds, as mentioned previously, were replaced by T-38s during 1989. Additionally, it should be noted that an exchange program with the F-117A exists and that at least one Royal Air Force pilot has been involved.

In a still-questioned turn of events surrounding the Panamanian dictatorship of Manuel Noriega, six F-117As of the 37th TFW were utilized for the first time in actual combat when two participated in a raid from Tegucigalpa in the Honduras against the Rio Hato barracks of the Panamanian army during *Operation Just Cause* on December 20, 1989. In an attempt to "stun, disorient, and confuse" Panamanian troops, the attacking aircraft were utilized to deliver a single modified 2,000 lb. BLU-109 laser-guided bomb supposedly within 150 meters of structures at the site without hitting

Jay Miller/Aerofax, Inc.

Fineness ratio of F-117A is quite good, in spite of its flat-plate design. Over-all length is similar to that of McDonnell Douglas F-15 "Eagle", and height above ground also is similar. Extreme sweep angle of vertical tail surfaces is readily apparent. Vertical tail surfaces are basically aluminum with RAM covering.

the buildings or causing them to collapse. Air Force spokesmen later attempted to justify use of the highly classified aircraft by claiming they were the only fighters in the Air Force inventory with the weapon delivery accuracy required for the job. Since the event, additional questions concerning the success of the attack have surfaced, as there is some indication that weapon delivery was not nearly as accurate as originally claimed.

The F-117A has been placed on alert status on at least two other occasions. An anti-terrorist raid was planned but later cancelled against Libya during April of 1986, and a similar attack against Syria also was planned and cancelled in retaliation for the 1983 bombing of the marine barracks in Lebanon. In both instances, there is some possibility that reported temporary relocating of at least two F-117As to bases in England was undertaken to accommodate such missions.

The 37th TFW's F-117As presently are supported by the Sacramento Air Logistics Center at McClellan AFB, California. This unit has established a depot at Air Force Plant 42 in Palmdale, California (also the location of Northrop B-2 final assembly) specifically to accommodate forthcoming F-117A overhaul requirements. At a nearby facility, also on the Palmdale airport, Lockheed maintains an update facility where F-117A systems are continuously upgraded to maintain technological currency.

Lockheed has continued to explore F-117A technology and design options and it is known that an advanced version of the aircraft, sometimes referred to as the F-117B, with more powerful engines and other changes providing better performance, has been proffered to the Air Force. Additionally, studies were conducted calling for a two-seat trainer derivative, but to date, nothing is known to have come of this. The general success of the transition program into the single-seat aircraft is thought effectively to have killed the trainer option.

F-117A serial numbers include:

80-0780/-0792	82-0798/-0808	84-0819/-0829
80-0793/-0797	83-0809/-0818	85-0830/-0839

The Department of Defense has acknowledged officially that total F-117A program costs for the 59 aircraft currently ordered is $6.56 billon. This figure is comprised of $2 billion for development and $4.27 billion for procurement and $295.4 million for construction of support facilities, etc. The cost per aircraft works out at $111.2 million. As of this writing, 58 of the 59 aircraft on order have been delivered, and the final aircraft will be delivered by the fall of 1990.

CONSTRUCTION AND SYSTEMS:

Fuselage: Conventional aluminum construction with plate-like RAM attached externally via epoxy adhesive. Quadruple-redundant fly-by-wire flight control system is fed environmental data via four RCS-optimized composite construction pitot assemblies mounted on nose. Two pitots are mounted on the starboard side, one is mounted centrally, and the remaining unit is mounted on the port side. All communications, EW, and other antennas and protuberances are either retractable or removeable. Optional radar reflector assembly and night flying lights can be bolted to the outside of each engine nacelle when non-combat operations in a civilian environment are required.

Cockpit: Conventional single-seat configuration with McDonnell Douglas ACES II (Advanced Capability Ejection Seat) ejection seat under a single-piece, hydraulically-actuated, aft-hinged, five-transparency canopy. Environmental control system identical to that utilized in Lockheed C-130. Communications radios and Honeywell inertial navigation system common to other aircraft. Sophisticated navigation/attack system is integrated with avionics suite. Displays consist of main central CRT on front panel and two peripheral smaller CRTs; minimal analog instrumentation primarily emergency back-up. Controls are conventional with centrally-mounted stick and rudder pedals interfaced with F-16-type quadruple redundant fly-by-wire system. Conventional, non-Raster heads-up-display is mounted above instrument panel combing.

Canopy transparencies are laminated and incorporate a gold film coating specifically optimized to lower radar returns from the cockpit. Additionally, the panels around the canopy area are given serrated edges to reflect energy at angles away from the beaming radar's receiver. Though not integral with the cockpit, it should be noted that detailed planning for missions into heavily defended target areas is accomplished by an automated mission planning system developed specifically to optimize the F-117A's capabilities.

Wings: Conventional aluminum construction materials with slab surfaces optimized to conform to computer-generated RCS specification. RAM materials applied in sheet form with smaller areas spray-covered. Conventional hydraulically-boosted elevons for pitch/roll control and hydromechanically actuated flaperons are fitted. W-shaped trailing edge design is optimized to conform to RCS equations. Wings are removable, but only with significant effort. Rumors pertaining to F-117A common transportability via C-5A/B remain unverified, but regardless, wing disassembly is not optimized for quick turnaround. Fuel tanks are integral with design.

Tail Surfaces: V-type design with double-diamond airfoil optimized for low RCS. Construction primarily aluminum (there are plans, however, to change to thermoplastic graphite composites). Covered with RAM. Prism-like cross-section. Hydraulically-actuated slab surfaces work in yaw mode only and do not contribute to pitch control.

Landing Gear: Heavy-duty conventional tricyle oleo-pneumatic configuration. Gear retraction direction is forward with all three gear assemblies. Main gear have a slight inward angular motion during the retraction process. All three gear wells are covered with prism-type RAM-surfaced doors. Doors are hydraulically assisted during the closing process in order to assure tight fit. Bendix carbon heat-sink brakes are the same as those utilized on the McDonnell Douglas F-15. Anti-skid is integral with brake system. A special all-black, ring-type drag chute and associated housing (with split cover doors) are mounted in the empennage area between the vertical tail surfaces. An arresting hook for use in emergencies is ventrally mounted in an enclosed well under empennage.

Powerplant: Two General Electric F404-GE-F1D2 two-shaft, augmented low-bypass-ratio turbofans. Engines are not afterburner equipped but generally are similar to other F404s in configuration and installation. Fan is three-stage type with a bypass ratio of 0.34. Airflow is 142 lbs./sec. (64.4 kg.). The high-pressure compressor is a seven-stage unit with an over-all pressure ratio of 25:1. The combustion chamber is a single-piece annular design. The high-pressure turbine is a single-stage unit with air-cooled blades. The low-pressure turbine is also a single-stage unit. Maximum diameter is 34.8 in. (880 mm). Maximum sea level thrust rating is 10,800 lbs. Oversize intake with structural splitter assembly has an electrically de-iced composite construction grid with a roughly 3/4" x 1-1/2" cell dimension. This serves to deflect incoming (10 centimeter wavelength/3GHz/E-band) radar-generated energy away from the highly reflective engine compressor section first stage turbine blades. The "platypus" exhaust duct assembly is an extremely wide slot (approx. 62 in.) with an extended and upward-angled lower lip. It is optimized to spread the exhaust plume and increase the rapidity of the ambient cool air mix. The lower lip serves to reduce the angular viewing window into the exhaust proper. This lip not only lowers aft quadrant RCS, but also contributes to lowering of the aircraft IR signature. Part of the vaned exhaust nozzle system (12 slots each side) includes the injection of cool air routed from a slot in front of the intakes that when mixed with the exhaust gases, effectively lowers the over-all temperature of the exhaust plume. A large, downward-retracting-auxiliary inlet door is located on top of each engine nacelle. Fuel consumption from "wet" wing tanks at cruise speed and altitude is approximately 3,000 lbs. an hour. Fuel capacity is approximately 1,850 gals. and fuel type is conventional JP-4. Aircraft is inflight refuelable with a dorsally-mounted receiver aft of cockpit area and

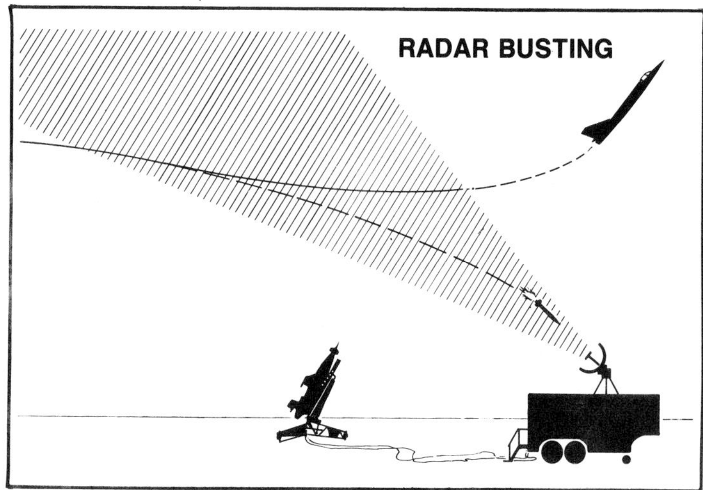

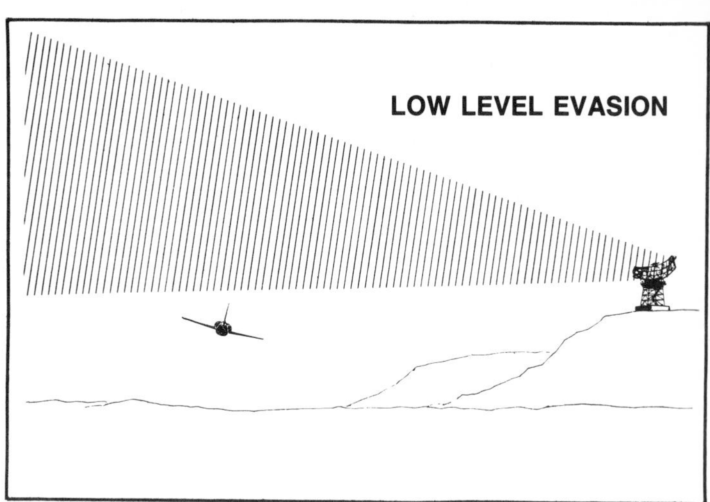

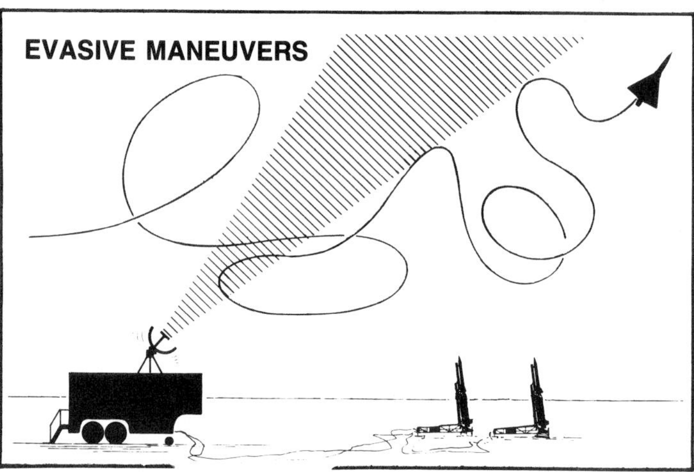

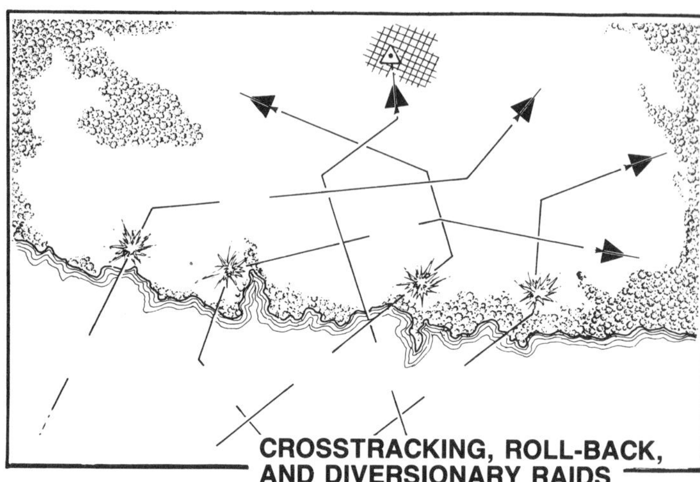

between engine bays. Refueling receptacle is illuminated for night operations by small floodlight mounted at apex of canopy dome assembly and is covered by a single door.

Weapons/Sensors: Forward-looking Texas Instruments IR and downward-looking IR sensors are mounted separately with former permanently affixed behind an IR-transparent covering just ahead of and below the windscreen and the latter mounted under the fuselage (on its starboard side) behind another fixed transparency. Laser tracker/designator is mounted in same compartments and is integral with FLIR/DLIR. Weapon bay with dual hinged, hydraulically actuated doors is capable of accommodating up to 5,000 lbs. Normal maximum payload complement is two 2,000 lb. bombs though single-bomb payloads are common. Most weapons are of the laser-guided variety and include bombs, missiles, and nuclear weapons. A small family of F-117-dedicated weapons with improved accuracy and possibly some stealth features has been developed, but no information is available. Some reports indicate that air-to-air capabilities have been explored.

RADAR:

A BRIEF HISTORY

Low observable stealth technology, as personified by the Lockheed F-117A, is the end product of the effect radar (ra[dio] d[etecting] a[nd] r[anging]) technology has had on the ability of such systems to detect and locate targets for destruction. Steady improvements in the power and accuracy of radar have reached a technological zenith during the past two decades that has resulted in very precise track-and-destroy capabilities. The latter have far outstripped more conventional countermeasures systems and as a result, extraordinary responses have been required to move the odds back in favor of the target.

The actual development of radar as we know it today can trace its roots back to 1886 when a German by the name of Heinrich Hertz verified Maxwell's electromagnetic theory by showing that shortwave (60 centimeters in length) radiation could be reflected from metallic and dielectric bodies. This event was followed, nearly two decades later, by fellow German Christian Huelsmeyer's work wherein radio waves were purposefully reflected from large ships at sea in an attempt to develop a proximity warning system allowing ships to maintain knowledge of each other's location during bad weather and/or at night. Still later, the technology generated by these experiments was found to be applicable to weather forecasting, as it was discovered by Britain's Sir Robert Watson-Watt that the electro-magnetic activity in storms could be detected by basically the same equipment. It was in fact Hertz, again, who conceived the idea of a directional loop antenna to take advantage of the phenomenon, and thus permit the relatively precise location of bad weather and its general direction of movement.

Interest in electro-magnetic wave propagation phenomenon had, by the early 1900s, spread worldwide. Two U.S. scientists, Gregory Breit and Merle Tuve of the Carnegie Institute in Washington, D.C., had spent considerable time developing equipment that was optimized to transmit signals over very long ranges by propagation of electro-magnetic energy through the atmosphere. One end product of this was a transmitter pulsing system that permitted them not only to broadcast, but to receive the resulting echo. Their formula, which simply was the time between the end of a transmission and the reception of an echo signal beamed upward and multiplied by the speed of radio waves (300,000,000 meters per second) and divided by two, became the principle of pulsing radio transmission and reception which later became the very basis for all future radar systems.

Integral with these developments came the need to visually display the information that was being generated and received. During 1897, Germany's Ferdinand Braun created the first, crude cathode ray tube (CRT), and over the following two decades, work on the basic principles of this seminal device led to a unit, revealed during 1923, that was applicable to what now were becoming the earliest forms of contemporary radar. Coincident to the work on the CRT, a diode-type generator, called a magnetron and capable of very short wave-lengths, was developed by Hull of General Electric; Sir Robert Watson-Watt patented a thunderstorm location-type radar with a range of about 400 miles and an accuracy in azimuth of 1°; Guglielmo Marconi, during June of 1922, released a paper urging the development of "short wavelengths" for purposes of object detection by radio; and some success was realized by scientists in various parts of the world in developing equipment that could generate the frequencies Marconi had suggested. Regardless of the successes enjoyed experimentally in laboratories around the world, a basic problem remained in that it was impossible to develop significant amounts of power at very high frequencies without resorting to extraordinarily large antennas.

In an act of serendipity during the 1930s, a U.S. Naval Research Laboratory scientist, while experimenting with the propagation of radio waves during a field test, had an aircraft pass accidentally through his equipment's radio beam. He immediately noticed that the energy reflected by the aircraft had caused a change (and in fact, an increase) in received signal strength. An intensive investigation followed and the result was a radio wave propagation system that permitted the detection of an aircraft at distances approaching fifty miles. This proved to be the first U.S. use of such devices for aircraft locating.

The U.S. Naval Research Laboratory effort was a credible step in the right direction, but simply detecting an aircraft did not provide any insight into its altitude, its velocity, or its direction of travel. While work continued on solving this problem through the development of high-power, high-frequency systems, during 1935, Sir Robert Watson-Watt was contacted by the Royal Navy and asked to explore the possibility of developing a electro-magnetic death ray that would destroy a target by elevating its temperatures to combustion level. This study resulted in a negative assessment by Watson-Watt, but consequently, it was determined that it might be possible to ring England with transmitter/receiver units that would result in an effective warning system to prevent a surprise attack from the air.

Though the basic idea of being able to send radio waves through a gas-filled tube had been placed on paper by Lord Rayleigh during 1897, it wasn't until 1936 that scientists at various research institutions around the world were able to transmit radio waves under such conditions for the first time. One of the surprises of this research was the realization that there was a tenfold increase in the amount of power being transmitted. Over the following four years, this concept was further explored and perfected, and along with the development of tuned circuits (cavity resonators), laid a solid foundation for truly effective radar units.

By 1937, the U.S. Navy had installed a crude 200 MHz (MegaHertz) radar in one of its ships, but the unit proved cumbersome, terribly underpowered, and decidedly unproductive. Technology leaps rapidly followed, however, including the development by the Varian Brothers of the klystron oscillator tube. This unit proved ideal for radar use, and later permitted the development of a one-watt-at-10-centimeters-frequency oscillator by Sperry Gyroscope Company.

With sufficient power at high frequencies now remaining as the last barrier, a team of researchers headed by M.L.H. Oliphant of Britain, during 1939, initiated an intense research effort that eventually resulted in a solution. By combining the Hull magnetron with the Hansen tuned circuits inside a diode in a manner creating a series of segmented sections, at least 10 kW of power at 10 centimeters frequency was generated for the first time in history. From this, rapid progress in legitimate radar technology became possible, and by 1940, similar activity, boosted by a British technology transfer, had gotten underway in the U.S.

Once the basic mechanical elements of radar were understood, the science of radar detection moved forward with little hindrance. From land and ship based units, radar technology moved ahead so rapidly that size reductions permitted installation first in bomber-size aircraft, and later in fighters. Radar technology eventually resulted in the design and development of systems with ranges measured in thousands of miles, accuracy measured in inches, and a multiplicity of capability that has today resulted in a tool with extraordinary versatility.

It is beyond the scope of this booklet to cover all of these advances in detail, but suffice it to say that both ground-based and airborne radar systems became feasible, operational use of radar played a key role in the outcome of many major and minor battles during World War II, Korea, and virtually every other conflict of any note up to the present time, and new and improved radar systems continue to find a variety of uses in virtually every field of endeavor.

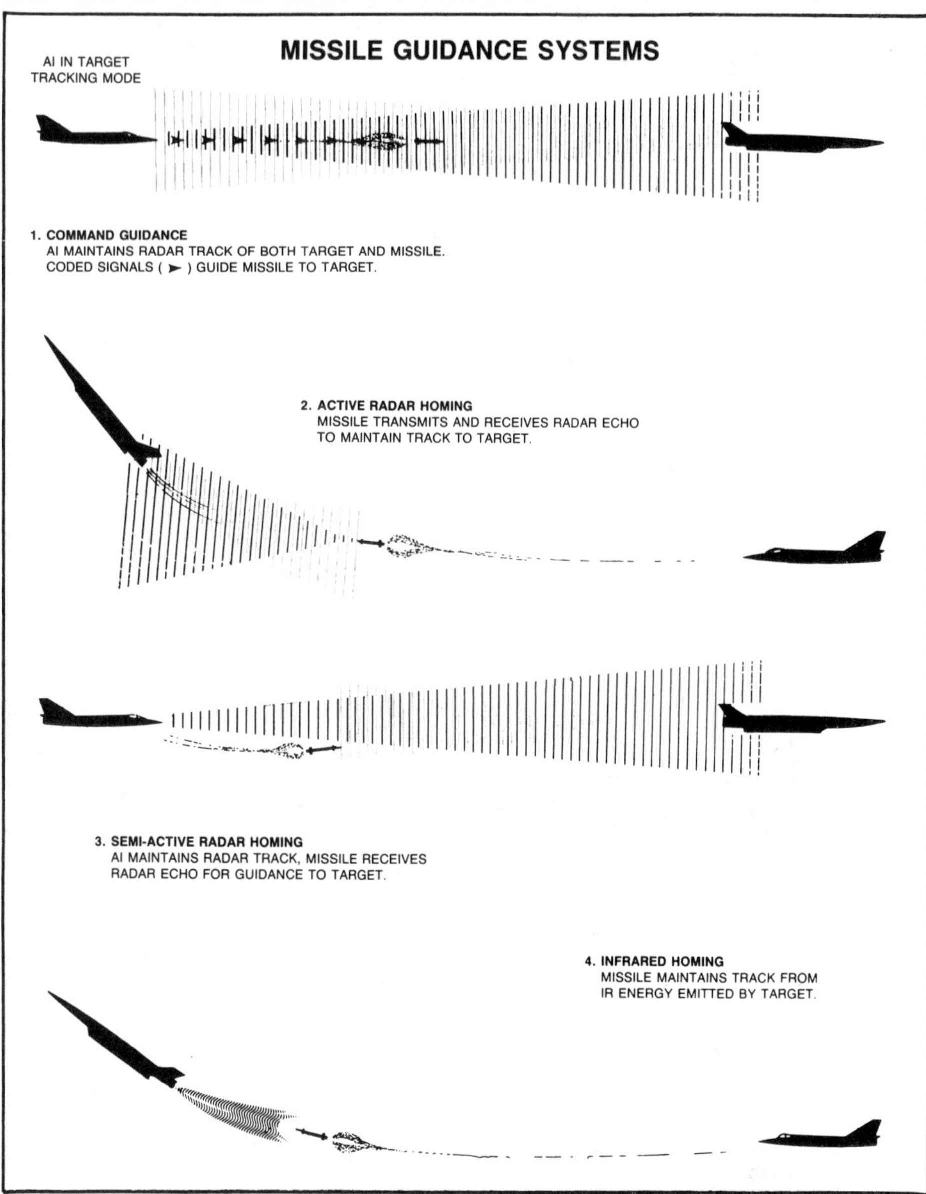

MISSILE GUIDANCE SYSTEMS
AI IN TARGET TRACKING MODE
1. COMMAND GUIDANCE
AI MAINTAINS RADAR TRACK OF BOTH TARGET AND MISSILE.
CODED SIGNALS (➤) GUIDE MISSILE TO TARGET.
2. ACTIVE RADAR HOMING
MISSILE TRANSMITS AND RECEIVES RADAR ECHO
TO MAINTAIN TRACK TO TARGET.
3. SEMI-ACTIVE RADAR HOMING
AI MAINTAINS RADAR TRACK, MISSILE RECEIVES
RADAR ECHO FOR GUIDANCE TO TARGET.
4. INFRARED HOMING
MISSILE MAINTAINS TRACK FROM
IR ENERGY EMITTED BY TARGET.

Applications include:

Civil sector: weather avoidance, navigation (area navigation, radar altimeters, radar beacons, distance measuring equipment, air traffic control beacons), maritime surveillance (search and rescue, ice patrol, oil slick detection), high resolution mapping, and sounding.

Space flight: landing aid, rendezvous aid, and mapping and sounding.

Military: navigation (blind low-altitude flight, special beacon applications, radar map-matching, precision velocity update, precision position update, forward-looking altitude measurement, Doppler navigation, landing guidance), early warning and sea surveillance, fighter/interceptor mission (search, raid assessment, target identification, fire control), missile guidance (command, beam riding, target seeking), air-to-ground operations (air-to-ground weapon delivery, stand-off surveillance of ground forces, reconnaissance), air-to-surface naval applications (anti-shipping, anti-submarine warfare), proximity fuzes, and countermeasures (passive countermeasures, jamming, deceptive countermeasures, counter-countermeasures).

PRINCIPLES OF OPERATION

The external appearance of a radar unit is dominated by its antenna which in most radars is some form of articulated parabolic reflector. The radar antenna can also be a fixed array of many small radiating elements (sometimes in the thousands) operating in unison to produce the desired radiation characteristics. Array antennas have the advantage of greater flexibility and more rapid beam steering than mechanically-steered reflector antennas because the beam movement can be accomplished by electrically changing the relative phase at each element of the antenna. High power can be radiated since a separate transmitter can be applied at each element. Additionally, the flexibility and speed of an array antenna make it necessary in some instances to control its function and analyze its output by automatic data processing equipment rather than more simple formats involving display devices.

Radars generally operate within the microwave portion of the electromagnetic spectrum, typically from around 200 MHz (1.5 meters wavelength) to around 35,000 MHz (8.5 millimeters wavelength)—though there are a decidedly large number of exceptions. The span between the two extremes is generally broken down into bands which are as follows:

SAM USING MISSILE AND TARGET TRACKING

KILL POINT

(360° ROTATION)

TECHNIQUE-1
SAM USING SEPARATE MISSILE AND TARGET TRACKING RADAR

SAM MISSILE LAUNCHER

MISSILE GUIDANCE

MISSILE TRACKER

3

5

1

INITIAL INFORMATION ACQUISITION RADAR

4

2

TARGET TRACKER

COMPUTER

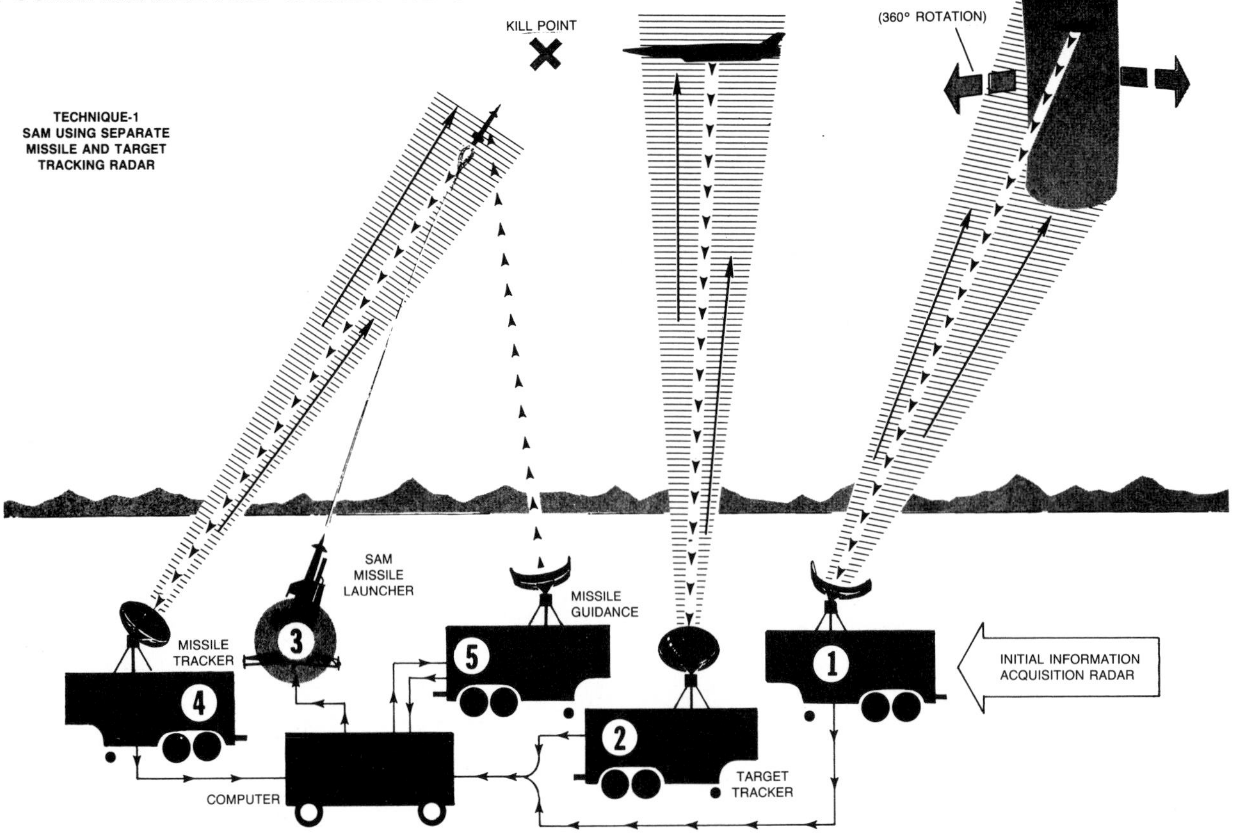

SAM USING TRACK-WHILE-SCAN

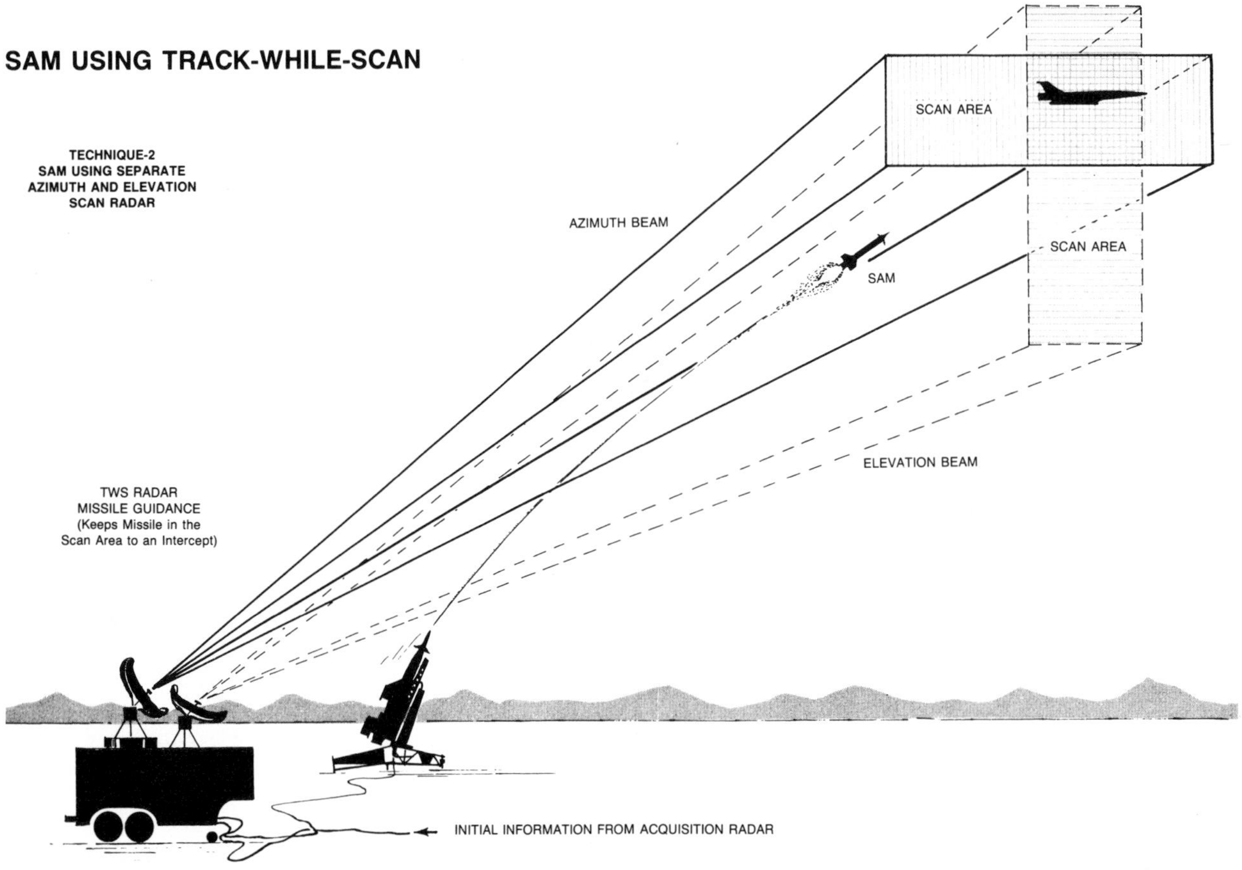

SCAN AREA

TECHNIQUE-2
SAM USING SEPARATE AZIMUTH AND ELEVATION SCAN RADAR

AZIMUTH BEAM

SCAN AREA

SAM

ELEVATION BEAM

TWS RADAR
MISSILE GUIDANCE
(Keeps Missile in the Scan Area to an Intercept)

INITIAL INFORMATION FROM ACQUISITION RADAR

Jay Miller/Aerofax, Inc.

Undersurface of F-117A essentially is flat in central area, but faceting does occur in conjunction with wing and fuselage node lines. Aircraft flies on lifting body principle. Protuberances under wings are fairings for main gear tires. Wing leading edge is straight from nose to wingtips. Airfoil is totally unconventional.

Jay Miller/Aerofax, Inc.

F-117A cockpit arrangement forces pilot to sit relatively high. View from cockpit is considered good, though limited in terms of aft vision. Ingressing and egressing requires special articulated boarding ladder. Transparencies have gold film laminate to lower radar return of cockpit area. Cockpit framing also contributes to low RCS.

Jay Miller/Aerofax, Inc.

F-117A auxiliary blow-in doors, visible on top side of engine nacelle area just to the rear of the intakes, provide additional air during taxiing and static powerplant runs. Placement of blow-in doors gives some insight into location of engine compressor face relative to intakes, and size of intake tunnel area.

Jay Miller/Aerofax, Inc.

F-117A perspective changes considerably from position to position around aircraft. Flat-plating of design is broken only by node intersects. The only noticeable blending that takes place is at the wing root at about mid-span.

Band	Frequency
A	0 to 250 MHz
B	250 to 500 MHz
C	500 MHz to 1 GHz
D	1 to 2 GHz
E	2 to 3 GHz
F	3 to 4 GHz
G	4 to 6 GHz
H	6 to 8 GHz
I	8 to 10 GHz
J	10 to 20 GHz
K	20 to 40 GHz
L	40 to 60 GHz
M	60 to 100 GHz

The basic principles upon which radar systems function are much older than most hardware specialists would lead us to believe. In fact, nature, for literally hundreds of thousands of years, has had operable sensors on line that function very much in concert with radar as we know it today. The bat, which uses an echo-locating system of extraordinary sophistication, determines its proximity to a target (or obstacle) by emitting high frequency (approx. 40 kHz) sound pulses. As these sound waves move outward, they contact any solid object in their path. Sound thus reflected from an object returns in part to the bat's ears. By calculating the amount of time between the emission of the sound and its reflection back to it's eardrum, the bat's brain is able to determine very precisely both how far away and exactly where a target or obstacle is located.

Radar works on essentially this same principle, only rather than detecting sound waves, it emits and detects radio waves in certain segments of the electro-magnetic spectrum. As radio waves are reflected in many different directions from most solid objects just like sound waves, usually a detectable portion is reflected back in the direction of the originating source. Thus if a radar generates electro-magnetic energy, a small amount, after contacting a solid object (target), will be reflected directly back.

Electromagnetic energy is just one of several energy forms. The analogous process of transmitting torque (mechanical energy) from a motor (source) to a wheel (load) through a shaft (medium) physically illustrates the transmission of radio waves (electromagnetic energy) from a transmitter to a receiver through the atmosphere or space.

Traveling electromagnetic energy is composed of two components: an electric field and a magnetic field. The two component fields travel through the medium together and in phase with each other. They are mutually perpendicular and perpendicular to the direction of travel.

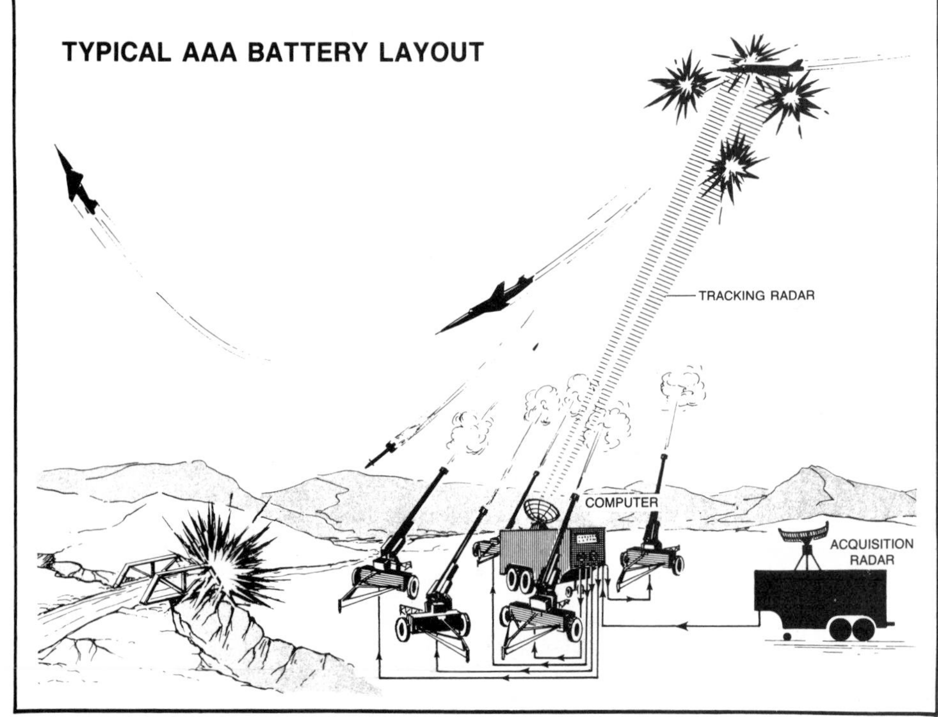

Terminology relating to this concept is as follows:

RF—Radio Frequency

Radio Wave Propagation—refers to the movement of radio waves through any medium.

Period of Oscillation—is the time in seconds required to complete one cycle of the oscillation.

Frequency—is the number of cycles completed in one second. The unit of frequency measurement for the electromagnetic spectrum is the Hertz (Hz).

Wavelength—is the distance the wave front will travel in the time of one cycle. If this energy could be photographed, the wavelength would represent the length of one complete cycle in space.

Amplitude of Oscillation—is a measure of the maximum displacement of the wave from its null or undisturbed condition.

Velocity of Propagation—of electromagnetic energy is approximately 300,000,000 meters (186,000 miles) per second. Thus ranging times generally are expressed in millionths of a second (microseconds). A 10 microsecond transit time, for instance, indicates a range of 1.5 kilometers.

Amplitude Modulation (AM)—consists of varying the amplitude of the RF energy wave in accordance with the changes in an imposed signal.

Frequency Modulation (FM)—consists of varying the frequency of the RF energy wave in accordance with the changes in an imposed signal. The information is represented by the rate and amount of frequency change.

Phase Modulation—consists of varying the phase of the RF energy wave in accordance with the changes of the imposed signal without changing the amplitude. The effects are similar to frequency modulation.

Pulse Modulation—consists of grouping the RF energy wave into specified pulses. The information is carried by a change in amplitude, number, and/or duration of the pulses.

Conveniently, the atmosphere (and the vacuum of space) is almost completely transparent to that part of the electromagnetic spectrum utilized for radio wave transmission. Accordingly, radio waves generated by radar have the attribute of being able to provide imagery of reflecting objects no matter what the general atmospheric conditions.

By transmitting radio waves and listening for their echoes, a radar can detect objects day or night and in all kinds of weather. By concentrating the transmitted waves into a narrow beam, it can determine direction. And by measuring the transit time of the waves, it can measure range.

To find a target, the radar beam is repeatedly swept through a search scan. Once detected, the target may be automatically tracked and its relative velocity computed on the basis of either periodic samples of its range and angular position obtained during the scan or continuous data obtained by training the antenna on the target. In the latter case, the target's echoes must be singled out in range and/or Doppler frequency, and some means such as lobing must be provided to sense angular tracking errors.

Because of Doppler effect, the radio frequencies of the echoes a radar receives are shifted in proportion to the reflecting object's range and its movement rate changes. By sensing these shifts, a radar can not only directly measure target closing rates, but reject clutter and differentiate between ground return and moving vehicles above or on the ground. It can even measure its own velocity.

Since radio waves are scattered in different amounts by different features of the terrain, a radar can also be used to map the ground.

Through synthetic array techniques, maps of near photographic detail can be made.

In its basic form, a radar consists of five elements: a radio transmitter, a radio receiver tuned to the transmitter's frequency, two antennas (one for transmitting and one for receiving) and a display unit. The transmitter detects a target by generating radio waves and the receiver picks up the reflected echoes. If a target is detected, it is indicated by some form of imagery on the display unit.

In practice, the transmitter and receiver generally share a common antenna. To avoid problems with reception interference, the radio waves usually are transmitted in pulses, and the receiver is turned off during the transmission events. Additionally, in order to allow radar to differentiate between targets in different directions as well as detect targets at dissimilar ranges, the antenna concentrates the radiated energy into a narrow beam—thus the generated radar energy is concentrated on only one target, or group of targets, at a time.

To find a target, the beam is scanned through a region in which targets might be expected. This is called a target space and the path of the beam in this space is called the search scan pattern. The region covered by the scan is called the scan volume or frame; the length of time the beam takes to scan the complete frame is called the frame time.

Radio waves essentially travel in a straight line. Consequently, for a radar to receive target echoes, the target must be in its line of sight. Even then, background electrical noise from the receiver output or ground clutter can sometimes mask the more important target return. Thus the strength of the target's echo is inversely proportional to the target's range to the fourth power ($1/R^4$). Consequently, as a target moves closer to the radar source, its echoes grow stronger. Detection ranges are dependent upon a number of factors including power of the transmitted waves; antenna size; target reflection characteristics; length of time the target is in the antenna beam during each search scan; number of search scans in which the target appears; wavelength of the radio waves; and background noise or clutter strength.

Transit time of a radar's electromagnetic energy is most simply deduced by measuring the time delay between the transmission of a pulse and the reception of the return echo. This method, called pulse-delay ranging, allows measurements to targets with an accuracy that can be measured in feet. A more sophisticated alternative method varying the frequency of the transmitted wave and permitting the observation of the lag time between modulation and the corresponding modulation of the echo has been developed for radar units that transmit continuously or generate pulses that are too close together to permit pulse-delay ranging.

In most airborne radar systems, the direction of a target is provided in terms of the angle between the line of sight to the target and a horizontal reference direction such as north, or the longitudinal axis of the aircraft's fuselage. This angle subsequently is resolved into its horizontal and vertical components, with the horizontal referred to as azimuth and the vertical referred to as elevation.

When only azimuth information is required, the antenna beam is generally given a narrow fan shape. When both azimuth and elevation are required, the beam is given a more or less conical shape. The latter is called a pencil beam and typically is is no more than 3° to 4° wide.

Though angular position can be determined based on the width of the beam, it is possible to obtain considerably more concise information by averaging return echo azimuths. For instance, if

Jay Miller/Aerofax, Inc.

F-117A's vertical tail surfaces are not faired and are attached directly to empennage upper surface. Empennage lower surface is trailing edge lip for engine exhaust nozzles and has noticeable upward curve.

Jay Miller/Aerofax, Inc.

Flat plate angles were determined by computer and are optimized for minimal radar return when aircraft is flown in a specific flight profile. Hexagonal shape of airfoil is discernible from this angle, as is straight leading edge.

echoes are received during the search scan at angles of 30° to 34°, the target's azimuth can be assumed to be approximately 32°. State-of-the-art radars, with advanced computer-integrated processing systems are capable of very precise target location.

In air-to-air combat, it frequently is necessary to track more than one target. This can be accommodated without stopping the search scan by utilizing a mode of operation now known as track-while-scan. Utilizing this technique, each target is continuously tracked on the basis of the periodic samples of range and angle obtained when the antenna beam sweeps across it. In the interim, if one target becomes a higher priority than the others, it is possible to stop the search scan and train the antenna on that specific target—thus transitioning to a single-target-track mode. However, keeping the antenna trained on the target automaticallly requires the sensing of angular pointing errors.

The latter, in early airborne radar systems, was initially sensed by rotating the beam so that its central axis swept out a small cone about the pointing axis (boresight line) of the antenna. If the target was on the boresight line (i.e., if there was no tracking error), its distance from the center of the beam would be the same throughout the conical scan and the amplitude of the received echoes would be unaffected. Since the strength of the beam falls off toward its edges, when a tracking error existed, the amplitude of the echoes was modulated by the scan. The amount of modulation thus indicated the magnitude of the tracking error and the point in each cycle of the scan at which the amplitude reached its minimum value indicated the direction of error.

Newer radars sense the error by sequentially placing the center line of the beam on one side and the other, and above and below the boresight line during reception only. This is called lobing and it is accomplished simultaneously by splitting the beam into four overlapping lobes during reception—which is called monopulse operation. Thus by continuously sensing the tracking errors with this last method and continuously correcting the pointing direction of the antenna so as to reduce the errors to zero, the antenna can be made to follow the movement of a target with extraordinary precision.

Consequent to this, while a target is being tracked, its range rate and angular rate (rate of movement of the line of sight to the target) also can be determined. In track-while-scan mode, for instance, the movement rates may be computed by dividing the changes in range and angular position from one scan to the next by determining the scan frame time. In single-target-track, the range rate may be determined more accurately from the continuously measured range and the angular rate may either be computed from the continuously measured angle or be measured directly by mounting gyros on the antenna sensitive to motion about the azimuth and elevation axes.

Knowing this information, it is possible to accurately assess the target's velocity relative to the

Lockheed/Eric Schulzinger and Denny Lombard

F-117A, 82-0807, *at Tonopah Test Range facility near Tonopah, Nevada. Base is located approximately 140 miles northwest of Las Vegas, Nevada next to the town of Tonopah. Contrary to the image presented, this and other static views of the F-117A were taken by Lockheed photographer Eric Schulzinger in sub-zero temperatures.*

Lockheed/Eric Schulzinger and Denny Lombard

Direct head-on view of ***F-117A, 82-0807,*** *at Tonopah Test Range facility. Extreme angularity of paneling in nose section is heavily accented. Offset red rotating beacon (one of two; the other is located dorsally) is visible on the starboard underside of the aircraft. Noteworthy are three-digits of serial number painted on nose gear strut.*

Lockheed/Eric Schulzinger and Denny Lombard

Inflight view of ***F-117A, 81-0796,*** *over what appear to be the Sierra Madre mountains of California. Extended UHF antenna and bolt-on red rotating beacon are noteworthy. Other antennas are mounted ventrally and are similarly retractable. Noteworthy also are the so-called 'platypus' exhaust nozzles.*

Lockheed/Eric Schulzinger and Denny Lombard

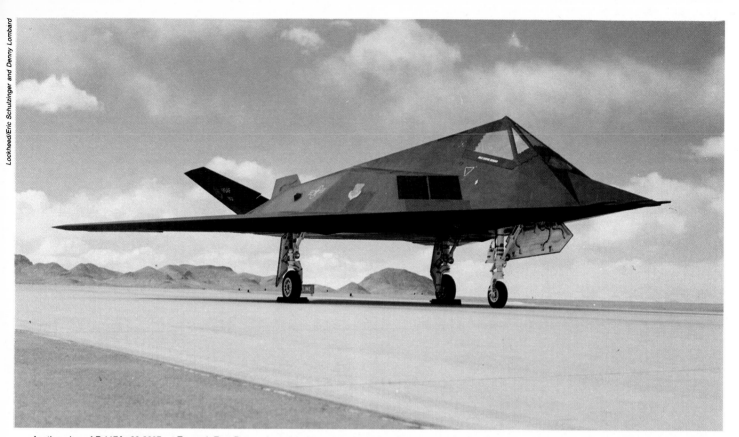

Another view of **F-117A, 82-0807,** at Tonopah Test Range. Angled position of landing gear door is unusual, but it compensates for slight inward retraction angle of main gear as it swings forward and up into well. Gold coloring of canopy transparencies is readily discernible, as is gold screen material protecting FLIR/laser designator unit.

Lockheed/Eric Schulzinger and Denny Lombard

An unidentified **F-117A** receives fuel from McDonnell Douglas KC-10A, 82-0191, of the 22nd ARW. F-117A refueling receptacle is located aft of the canopy, thus complicating piloting requirements. Receptacle apparently is integral with rotating door assembly. Night refueling requires use of small light at apex of canopy framing.

LOCKHEED F-117A, 82-0799

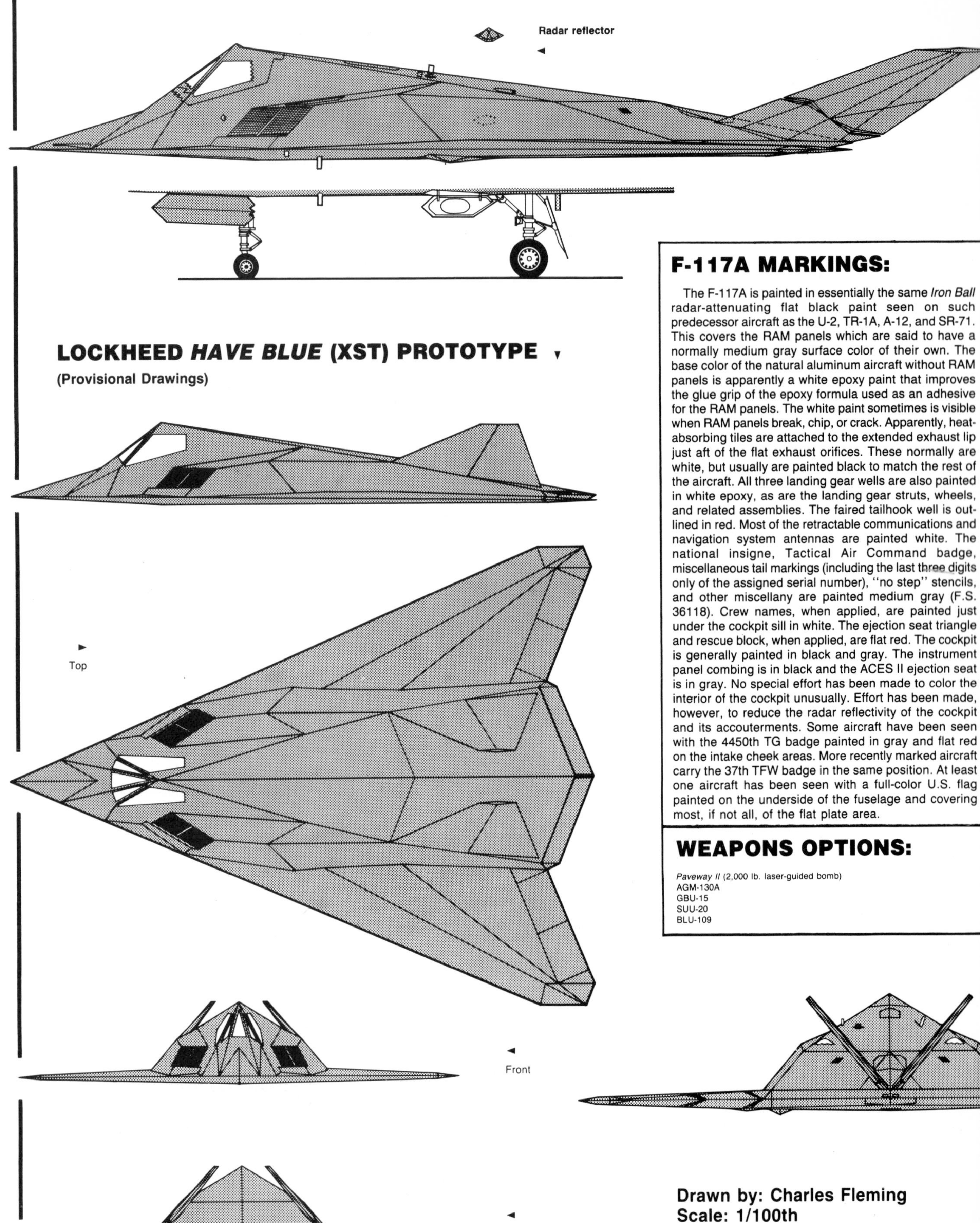

LOCKHEED *HAVE BLUE* (XST) PROTOTYPE

(Provisional Drawings)

F-117A MARKINGS:

The F-117A is painted in essentially the same *Iron Ball* radar-attenuating flat black paint seen on such predecessor aircraft as the U-2, TR-1A, A-12, and SR-71. This covers the RAM panels which are said to have a normally medium gray surface color of their own. The base color of the natural aluminum aircraft without RAM panels is apparently a white epoxy paint that improves the glue grip of the epoxy formula used as an adhesive for the RAM panels. The white paint sometimes is visible when RAM panels break, chip, or crack. Apparently, heat-absorbing tiles are attached to the extended exhaust lip just aft of the flat exhaust orifices. These normally are white, but usually are painted black to match the rest of the aircraft. All three landing gear wells are also painted in white epoxy, as are the landing gear struts, wheels, and related assemblies. The faired tailhook well is outlined in red. Most of the retractable communications and navigation system antennas are painted white. The national insigne, Tactical Air Command badge, miscellaneous tail markings (including the last three digits only of the assigned serial number), "no step" stencils, and other miscellany are painted medium gray (F.S. 36118). Crew names, when applied, are painted just under the cockpit sill in white. The ejection seat triangle and rescue block, when applied, are flat red. The cockpit is generally painted in black and gray. The instrument panel combing is in black and the ACES II ejection seat is in gray. No special effort has been made to color the interior of the cockpit unusually. Effort has been made, however, to reduce the radar reflectivity of the cockpit and its accouterments. Some aircraft have been seen with the 4450th TG badge painted in gray and flat red on the intake cheek areas. More recently marked aircraft carry the 37th TFW badge in the same position. At least one aircraft has been seen with a full-color U.S. flag painted on the underside of the fuselage and covering most, if not all, of the flat plate area.

WEAPONS OPTIONS:

Paveway II (2,000 lb. laser-guided bomb)
AGM-130A
GBU-15
SUU-20
BLU-109

Drawn by: Charles Fleming
Scale: 1/100th

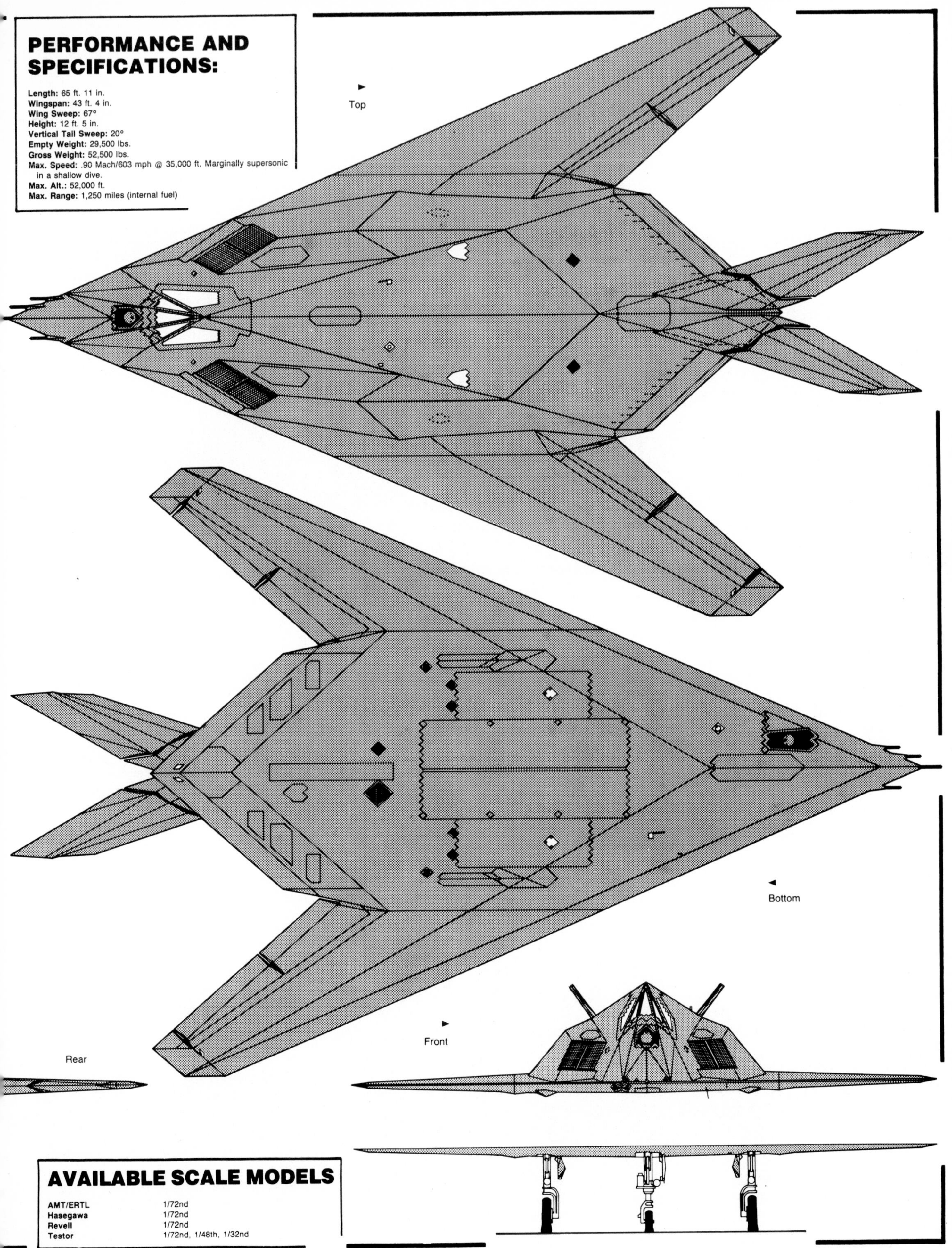

PERFORMANCE AND SPECIFICATIONS:

Length: 65 ft. 11 in.
Wingspan: 43 ft. 4 in.
Wing Sweep: 67°
Height: 12 ft. 5 in.
Vertical Tail Sweep: 20°
Empty Weight: 29,500 lbs.
Gross Weight: 52,500 lbs.
Max. Speed: .90 Mach/603 mph @ 35,000 ft. Marginally supersonic in a shallow dive.
Max. Alt.: 52,000 ft.
Max. Range: 1,250 miles (internal fuel)

AVAILABLE SCALE MODELS

AMT/ERTL	1/72nd
Hasegawa	1/72nd
Revell	1/72nd
Testor	1/72nd, 1/48th, 1/32nd

Jay Miller/Aerofax, Inc.

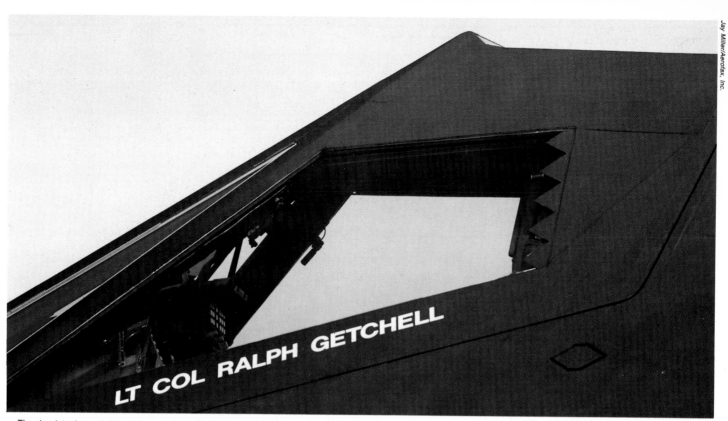

The view into the cockpit from the outside is effectively undisturbed by gold film laminate. Visible is HUD, HUD panel, and main instrument panel port CRT. Basic panel consists of two small CRTs surrounding a larger, central unit. Panel coloring is generally black. Other interior colors appear to consist of conventional grays.

Jay Miller/Aerofax, Inc.

Lockheed **F-117A, 80-0790,** shortly after its arrival at Nellis AFB, Nevada on April 21, 1990. This was the aircraft's first public showing. By the time of photo, all antennas had been retracted. Drag chute compartment doors remain open, however. Markings were specially applied for this event.

Jay Miller/Aerofax, Inc.

Lockheed **F-117A, 84-0828,** shortly ater its arrival at Nellis AFB, Nevada on April 21, 1990. Aircraft's 37th TFW markings, visible on the vertical tail, were specially applied for this event, as were the TR tailcode and related items. F-117As normally are flown only with serial numbers and national insignia visible.

Jay Miller/Aerofax, Inc.

Nose section markings are minimal. All are in white. Unusually, the ejection seat triangle also is in white. Coloration of gold film laminate in canopy transparencies is readily apparent. A similar effect can be seen on the intake and FLIR/DLIR/laser screens at certain angles.

Jay Miller/Aerofax, Inc.

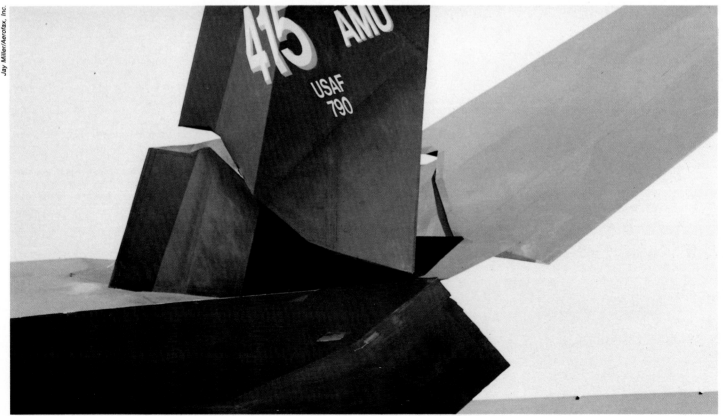

Empennage of **F-117A** is complex interfacing of several different planes. Airfoil section of V-tail surfaces is totally unorthodox. Somewhat jagged edge to upswept trailing edge lip is noteworthy. Visible lower left is red outline of tailhook compartment. Also visible is gray accent to white lettering.

Jay Miller/Aerofax, Inc.

Upward curve of empennage lower surface prevents ground-level viewing of exhaust. Consequently, it also limits infrared sensor viewing angle while aircraft is in the air. Upper decking channels cooling air to exhaust area.

Jay Miller/Aerofax, Inc.

Elevated view of aft fuselage area. Twelve exhaust duct assemblies are readily visible, as is upward curved lip extension. Asymetrical flap sag is noteworthy. Intersecting plates can be seen to always result in straight node lines.

Jay Miller/Aerofax, Inc.

Flat plate of fuselage undersurface is broken only by bomb bay door hinge fairings and miscellaneous access doors. Seal on virtually all of the latter items is exceptionaly tight to prevent radar reflection.

radar unit itself. The range rate, for instance, is the component of relative velocity along the line of sight. The angular rate multiplied by the range is the component normal to the line of sight. Adding the two vectorially provides relative velocity data.

Even in consideration of the above, it is possible, through what is known as Doppler effect, to extract still more data from radar echoes by sensing the shift in their radio wave frequency. Because of Doppler effect, the radio wave frequency of a moving radar's—or its target's—return echoes is generally shifted slightly relative to the frequency of the transmitted wave. This shift is proportional to the reflecting object's range rate. Consequently, by sensing a target's Doppler shift, or Doppler frequency, a radar can directly measure a target's range rate. Additionally, a radar can greatly expand its capabilities in other respects, as well, improving its ability to deal with background clutter, tracking moving ground targets, differentiating returns from rain and real targets, and determining its own velocity (i.e., the aircraft's relative ground speed), etc.

The different radar operation formats are as follows:

Continuous Wave Doppler Radar—This basic system consists of a transmitter, a receiver, an indicator, and appropriate antennas. The basic system cannot assess range. However, it is excellent for detecting the closing velocity of a target.

The transmitted RF energy is radiated, strikes the target, and returns to the receiver. The frequency of the returning RF echo is compared with the frequency of the transmitted energy. If the target is moving relative to the transmitter, the returning energy is at a different frequency—a Doppler shift. This difference in frequency is amplified, processed, and sent to the indicator as a target velocity.

Use of the basic Doppler is limited because of its inability to determine range or to detect targets with zero velocity relative to the radar transmitter. It also is difficult to obtain the high RF power required to produce detectable RF echoes from distant targets. This is true of all continuous wave systems.

Frequency Modulated Continuous Wave Doppler Radar—By modulating the frequency of the CW Doppler radar, it is possible to measure range and relative velocity. Two frequency changes are compared to give an indication of target velocity; the average frequency difference gives an indication of target range.

FM-CW Doppler radar still has the same power disadvantages of the basic Doppler since it too is a CW system. Thus the FM-CW radar provides both a range and velocity; however, as with the basic Doppler system, the velocity measured is limited to a relative velocity.

Pulsed Radar—To overcome the serious range limitations inherent in a CW system, the pulsed radar system was developed. It is designed to generate RF energy at extremely high peak power, while the average power remains relatively low. This makes long-range operation posssible. The increased range capability and adaptability to most search or tracking problems make the pulsed radar system the one generally used by military forces.

The transmitted RF energy strikes a target which re-radiates the energy in many directions. A small part of this energy is directed back toward the radar receiver. The receiver amplifies this echo (RF reflected energy), processes it into a video pulse of current or voltage, and displays the pulse on a CRT indicator.

The CRT presentation format is determined by the information desired. The CRT presentation must be coordinated with the antenna. The CRT may present a simple time base for the measurement of range (A scope); chart an area by tracing a "radar picture" of the surrounding terrain (PPI scope); display range and altitude (RHI scope); or "highlight" a target for tracking (G scope).

Pulse radar characteristics are described in the following terms:

Pulse Width (PW)—is the duration in time that the transmitter is actually transmitting RF energy. This duration is measured in microseconds. PW limits the radars minimum range. It also determines the ability of the radar to separate two targets having the same bearing.

Pulse Repetition Frequency (PRF)—is the number of RF pulses generated per second. PRF normally falls within the audio range (16 to 20,000 Hz). PRF determines the maximum range of the radar. The transmitter must remain quiet during the listening time (time that targets are received and displayed on the indicator).

Pulse Recurrence Time (PRT)—is the time it takes a radar to complete one cycle of operation (transmit a pulse, receive the echo, and prepare the transmitter for the next pulse). PRT is the reciprocal of PRF. The rotational speed of the radar's antenna is limited by the PRT.

Peak Power (Ppk)—is the maximum level of power produced for the duration of the PW.

Average Power (Pavg)—is the amount of continuous power that must be supplied by the DC power supply. Average power, like peak power, is measured in Watts.

Military radar systems can basically be broken down into three groups: (1) Indirect Threat Radars; (2) Direct Threat Radars; and (3) Non-Threat Radars. Each of these consists of the following:

Indirect Threat:

Early Warning (EW) or Long Range Radar (LRR)—is a high-power set used for long range detection of aircraft. Its main purpose is early detection as opposed to accuracy. Hence it is characterized by relatively long pulse widths (2 to 20 microseconds), low PRF (100 to 400 pulses per second), and frequencies in the range of 200 to 1,400 mHz. The long PWs allow the transmission of very high power (1 to 10 megaWatts). The low PRF allows very long listening times and ranges up to 300 nm are common.

The scan type used with early warning radars is circular. A narrow fan-shaped beam is rotated a full circle around a fixed vertical axis. Typically the beam can be shaped to about 2° of azimuth and 10° in elevation. This gives acceptable azimuth resolution and good altitude coverage. This fan-shaped beam is rotated slowly usually three to five rpm so that several successive pulses will hit and reflect from each target. Thus the data collection capability is limited by the PRF and the scan rate.

Acquisition Radar—is associated with ground weapon systems such as anti-aircraft artillery (AAA) or surface-to-air missiles (SAMs) and is a variation of the early warning radar. It is similar in fuction to the EW in that it provides range and azimuth information. This information is used as preliminary information for the target tracking radar. Range resolution is improved as is the azimuth resolution and data collection rate. These radars have shorter PWs (typically one microsecond), PRFs a little higher (perhaps 500 to 800 pulses per second), and more narrow beam widths. In addition, the sweep rate is increased to around 12 rpm. Of course, with the improvement in accuracy comes a sacrifice in range and total power. The maximum theoretical range drops to around 150 nm and the actual ranges are even less because of the power shortfall. These radars normally operate at high frequencies (2,700 to 3,500 mHz) to facilitate focusing of the beam into a more precise pattern.

Scott Newman

F-117A gear wells are painted in white epoxy paint. Gear wells are relatively free of accouterment, possibly in consideration RCS requirements. Gear doors are hydraulically boosted to ensure tight fit upon closing.

Height Finder Radars (HF)—The EW, Acquisition, and ASR provide azimuth and range information. One vital intercept parameter is missing with these units, however, and that's altitude. The HF radar supplies this information. It is similar in many respects to the EW radar except that the beam shape and scan type must be modified to provide a narrow beam (typically 1.5°) in the elevation and a wider sector (4°) in azimuth. This narrow fan-shaped beam then is nodded up and down in an arc from about 2° to 32°. The other characteristics of this radar include PW of 2 to 3 microseconds, and PRFs of 200 to 400 pulses per second, with an effective range of about 200 nm. The RF is again above 2,500 mHz so that the beam may be shaped into its characteristic pattern.

Ground Controlled Intercept—uses the combined information from the EW and HF radars which provide azimuth and elevation, and a double check of range. A site having both an EW and HF radar has a three-dimensional fix on a target and can thus vector an interceptor into the area.

"V" Beam—derives its name from the shape of its transmitted beam. Two fan-shaped beams similar to that of the EW radar beam are swept concurrently. One beam is vertical and the other is at some convenient angle. In addtion to range and azimuth from the vertical beam, a time difference between intercept echoes from the two beams on a target tells how far up the "V" the target is. This provides altitude information.

Direct Threat:

Gunlayer (GL)—is a relatively low-powered, precision radar using conical scan for tracking and either helical or spiral scan for acquisition. In conical scanning, the radar beam is made to describe the shave of a cone in space. The apex of this cone is located on the antenna and the angle of the cone is less than twice the width of the radar beam normally radiated. A target within the constraints of the beamed energy sends back a constant amplitude echo from all beams and the radar thus is said to be "locked-on" the target. If the target moves out of the area of overlap, returns of varying amplitude are sent back to the radar as the beam rotates through one complete cycle. A comparison of signal strengths creates an error signal and causes the antenna drive unit to move the antenna in the direction of the strongest return.

To isolate one target and increase the speed of gathering data, the conical scanning radar usually operates with a high PRF (1,000 to 2,000 PPS), narrow PW (0.5 to 1.5 microseconds), and highlights the target with its pencil beam. A complete set of azimuth and elevation data is received by the radar every revolution of the beam (approximately 1,800 rpm). This means that the maximum rate of gathering data is about 30 times per second. The RF is usually between 2,500 and 3,000 mHz to facilitate beam-shaping. The actual beam width can be reduced to less than 2° with an effective beam width less than 1/2°.

The small beam width of conical scan makes it ideal for tracking but relatively useless for acquiring the target. Using a helical or a spiral search pattern allows a large area to be searched with a pencil beam. As soon as the target is found, the radar transitions into the conical scanning track-mode. As a point of interest, transition time can be reduced by the use of a Palmer scan (the superimposition of conical scan onto one of the acquisition scans).

Airborne Intercept Radar (AI)—uses conical scan or monopulse for its tracking mode and either raster or spiral scan for target acquisition. Actually, the only difference between the conical scan used for AI operation and gunlayer operation is the RF. An airborne interceptor radar system usually operates above 8,500 mHz to reduce the physical size of the transmitter and receiver components.

The acquisition scan is necessary since the GCI resolution cell is so large. The spiral scan pattern is the same for gunlaying and airborne interceptors. Raster scan serves the same purpose as spiral scan and differs primarily in the scanning pattern. Palmer scan may be used to decrease transition time.

Surface-to-Air Missile Radar (SAM)—consists primarily of monopulse and track-while-scan systems. The monopulse system obtains sufficient information from each transmitted pulse to update its computers and reposition its antenna. Instead of scanning a single beam, the radar uses a minimum of four separate beams which transmit together but receive independently. By comparison of the energy returned in the beams, azimuth and elevation corrections can be made. The two advantages of this system over conical scan are its speed in gathering data and its ability to track a target even though there is a large amount of pulse-to-pulse fading.

The basic operation of the airborne monopulse

John Andrews

National insigne is visible on the underside starboard wing. In actual combat conditions it is said that all markings are removed form the aircraft. Additionally, all navigation lights, the rotating beacon, and related items are removed.

radar is identical to the SAM's; however, details are changed to make the system compatible with the over-all airborne weapons system.

Track-While-Scan (TWS)—is not a tracking radar in the usual sense. It produces two beams; an elevation sectoring beam and an azimuth sectoring beam. It is analogous to operating a collocated precision height-finder and air-surveillance radar. Each beam sectors a fixed quadrant and has the capability of displaying several targets simultaneously. The PRF usually is above 1,000 PPS and the sector rate is approximately 16 Hz. Updated azimuth and elevation data are obtained with each sector of the two beams. Since the antenna does not "highlight" the target, the system is unaffected by pulse fading.

Non-Threat:

Over-the-Horizon (OTH)—is principally employed as a missle launch detection system. By using an RF energy scatter system, the OTH radar can detect ionospheric disturbances caused by missile penetration.

Airborne Navigation—are high-frequency systems (above 8,500 mHz) that give a pictorial display of the territory below the aircraft. When used in conjunction with an associated computer, Doppler radar and astrotracker, the airborne navigation system is extremely accurate and reliable.

Side-Looking (SL or also Side-Looking Airborne Radar—SLAR)—are mapping radars that use the zero Doppler shift abeam the aircraft to create an extremely small "artificial aperture" (synthetic aperture). The radar returns are printed on film in rasters very similar to television. These rasters produce a continuous "strip photograph" of the area abeam the aircraft.

Space Surveillance (SS)—are low frequency radars (UHF band) with pulse widths in excess of 2,000 microseconds and peak power levels in excess of three megaWatts. To obtain the necessary accuracy, antenna diameters of 25 ft. are common. These radars can detect targets with a one-square-meter cross section out to 2,000 nm.

Air Surveillance (ASR)—are associated with most airports. Typically, the ASR is used for departure and approach control and as an acquisition radar for ground control approach. It is a relatively precise, short-range radar. PWs normally are less than one microsecond and PRFs are in excess of 1,000 pulses per second. Sweep rates are usually 12 to 20 rpm. Range is on the order of 50 to 90 nm. Frequencies of operation usually are between 2,700 and 2,900 mHz.

John Andrews

Faceting of undersurface of wing and fuselage is readily apparent in this early morning view taken at Tonapah Test Range. Offset lower rotating beacon and wingtip lights are readily visible.

ACRONYMS & ABBREVIATIONS:

AAA	anti-aircraft artillery
ACES	advanced capability ejection seat
ADP	advanced development projects
ADRAM	advanced radar absorbent material
AI	airborne intercept
ALCM	air-launched cruise missile
AM	amplitude modulation
ASR	air surveillance radar
ASV	air-to-surface-vessel
CRT	cathode ray tube
DARPA	defense advanced research projects agency
dB	decibel
DECM	defensive electronic countermeasures
DLIR	downward-looking infrared
ECM	electronic countermeasures
EW	early warning or electronic warfare
FLIR	forward-looking infrared
FM	frequency modulation
FM-CW	frequency modulation/continuous wave
FSD	full-scale development
GCI	ground control intercept
GHz	gigaHertz
GL	gunlayer
HARP	Halpern anti-radar paint
HF	height finder
Hz	Hertz
IR	infrared
IRAM	improved radar absorbent material
IRCM	infrared countermeasures
kW	kiloWatt
LRR	long-range radar
MHz	MegaHertz
nm	nautical miles
OTH	over the horizon
Pavg	average power
PPI	plan position indicator
Ppk	peak power
PRF	pulse repetition frequency
PRT	pulse recurrence time
PW	pulse width
Radar	ra(dio) d(etecting) a(nd) r(anging)
RCS	radar cross-section
RF	radio frequency
RHI	range-height indicator
SALT	strategic arms limitation talks
SAM	surface-to-air missile
SLAR	side-looking airborne radar
SS	space surveillance
TWS	track-while-scan
UHF	ultra-high frequency
XST	experimental, stealth, tactical

IN DETAIL:

Jay Miller/Aerofax, Inc.

F-117A nose is flat plate assembly like rest of aircraft. Canopy transparencies are laminates with gold film layer. Gold-colored screen over upper FLIR is noteworthy.

Jay Miller/Aerofax, Inc.

Canopy RCS details include angled plates on forward edge of canopy frame and on various transparency frame edges. Canopy is hydraulically raised and lowered.

Jay Miller/Aerofax, Inc.

Cockpit interior is fairly conventional. ACES II ejection seat, contrary to generally circulated information, is standard medium gray. Panel combing is black.

Jay Miller/Aerofax, Inc.

Canopy peak is faired light for illuminating dorsally-mounted inflight refueling receptacle during night operations. There are three locking latches on each side of canopy.

Jay Miller/Aerofax, Inc.

When closed, canopy fits snugly except where dog tooth edges overlap primary structure to prevent radar energy from penetrating and reflecting. FLIR unit fits underneath gold-colored screen just ahead of windscreen. FLIR and laser designator unit rotate into position when activated. Screen permits energy out, but not in.

Jay Miller/Aerofax, Inc.

Dome-like FLIR/laser unit is readily visible behind protective, non-reflective screen. Screen apparently is quite fragile and must be replaced with significant regularity.

Jay Miller/Aerofax, Inc.

Canopy framework, like rest of aircraft, is covered with RAM. Basic premise of canopy was to reduce radar return from cockpit, which historically is one of the best reflectors.

Jay Miller/Aerofax, Inc.

Special segmented boarding ladder has been developed to ingress and egress the F-117A. Noteworthy is protection provided on wing leading edge and cockpit railing.

Jay Miller/Aerofax, Inc.

Nose flat-plating is particularly pronounced. Noteworthy is the fact that there is no conventional boundary layer bleed system between fuselage side panels and intakes. Prism effect is considerably less pronounced under nose, but is considerably more linear. There is no leading edge break from nose to wingtips.

Jay Miller/Aerofax, Inc.

Four pitot-like assemblies feed environmental data to quadruple redundant fly-by-wire flight control system and instrumentation. Pitot assemblies are composite construction and apparently have been difficult to heat for deicing purposes. Diamond cross-section is the end product of RCS detailing.

Jay Miller/Aerofax, Inc.

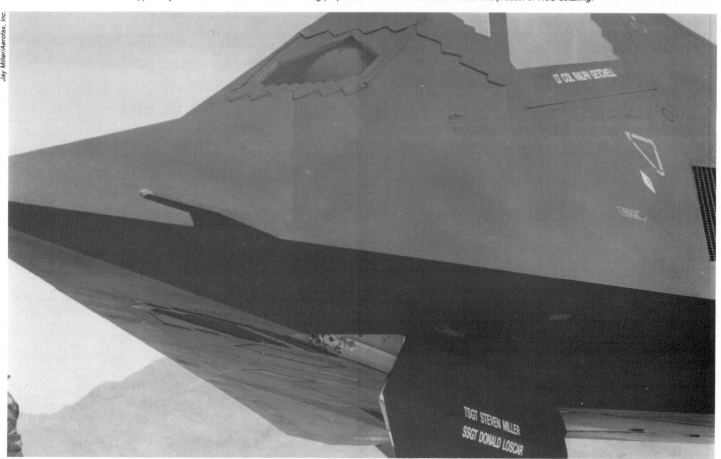

Centerline node begins at extreme tip of nose and continues to point under fuselage where it contacts flat plate area. Node then breaks and sets up nodes for first wing flat plate section forward of main spar. Geometry of design is extremely complex and is the result of work conducted utilizing a Cray computer.

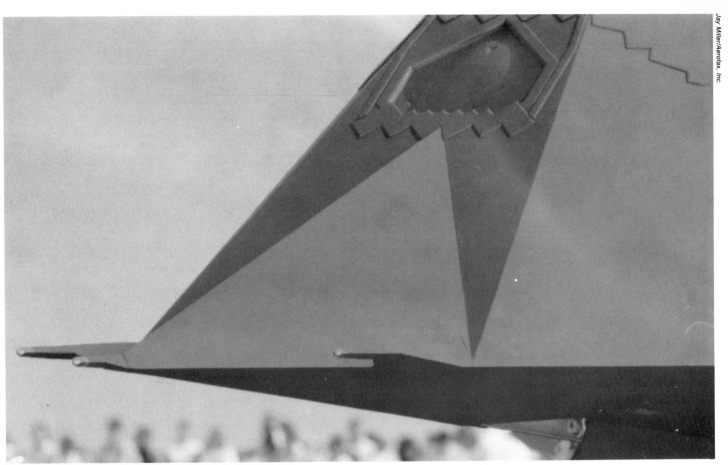

Jay Miller/Aerofax, Inc.

A total of four pitot assembles (three are visible here) are mounted assymetrically on nose leading edge section. Two pitot tubes protrude from the starboard leading edge, one is mounted on the extreme tip of the aircraft nose, and a single fourth pitot is mounted on the port leading edge.

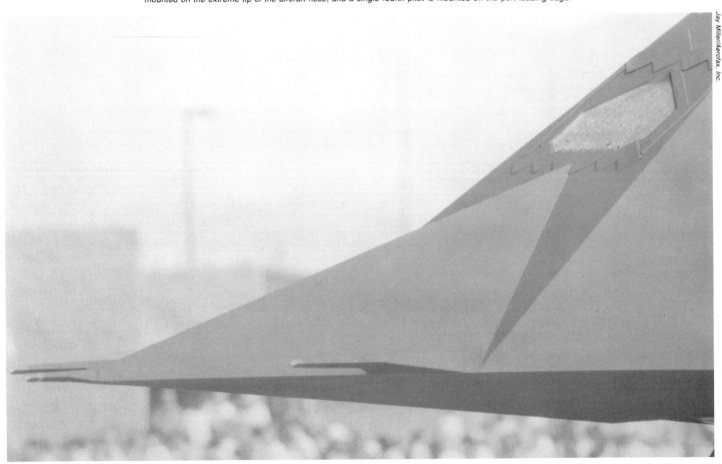

Jay Miller/Aerofax, Inc.

Nose tetrahedron assembly has sharp edges. Section is faired into flat plate into general cockpit area inside of which is mounted the FLIR/laser unit. The latter projects its energy through a gold-colored screen/mesh which some sources claim to be elastic. Screen/mesh is easily damaged by rain, insects and related objects.

Jay Miller/Aerofax, Inc.

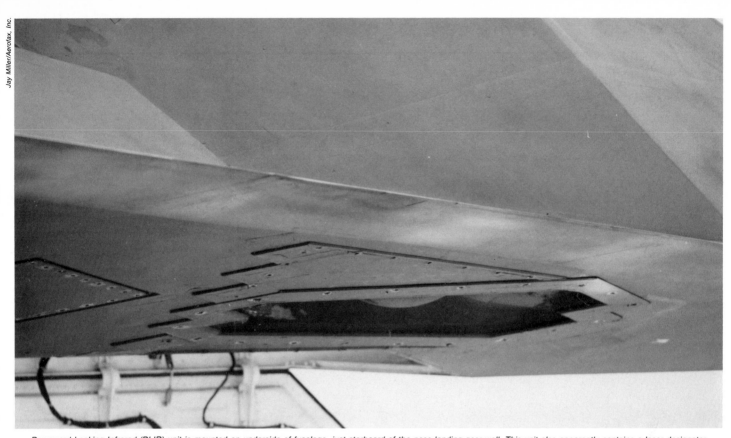

Downward Looking Infrared (DLIR) unit is mounted on underside of fuselage, just starboard of the nose landing gear well. This unit also apparently contains a laser designator assembly similar to that mounted in the upper FLIR compartment. Like the upper unit, the DLIR covering is a translucent gold-colored screen.

Jay Miller/Aerofax, Inc.

Basic aerodynamics of flat-plate design are a hindrance to high-performance. Aircraft is said to have attained supersonic speeds in a shallow dive, but only on rare occasions.

Jay Miller/Aerofax, Inc.

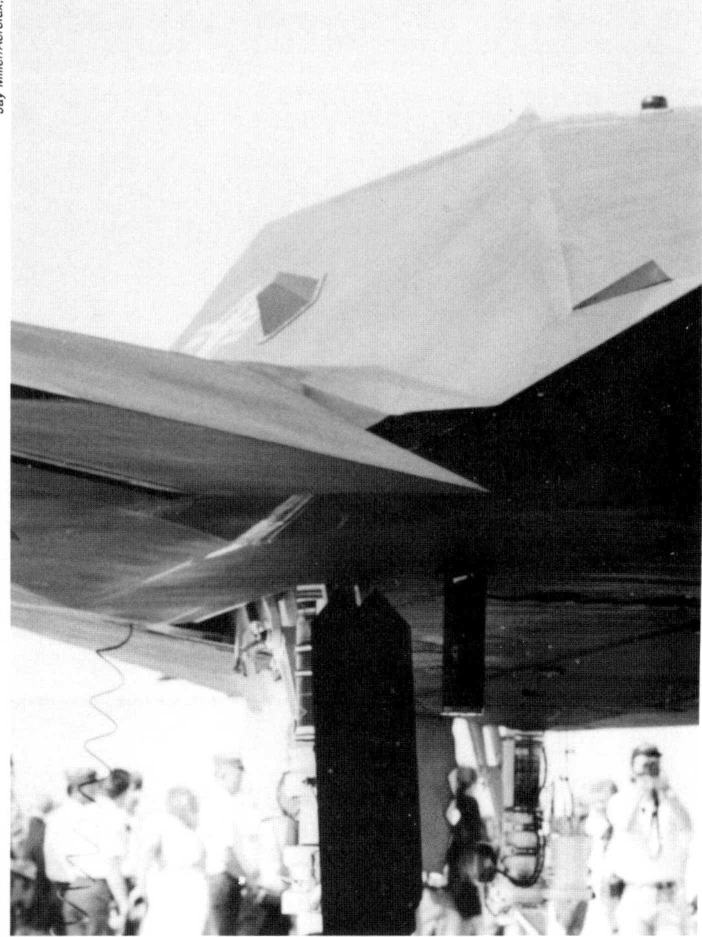

Trailing edge root extension is concession to inward angling of engine compartment flat plate area. Noteworthy is triangular piece projecting from exhaust lip extension.

Jay Miller/Aerofax, Inc.

Jay Miller/Aerofax, Inc.

Because the F-117A is optimized to provide an absolutely minimal radar return, it is often equipped with special radar reflectors on each engine compartment flat-plate, just above the wing root. These are easily removed and their mounting holes then can be filled with spray-on RAM. Photos show variations to mounting area.

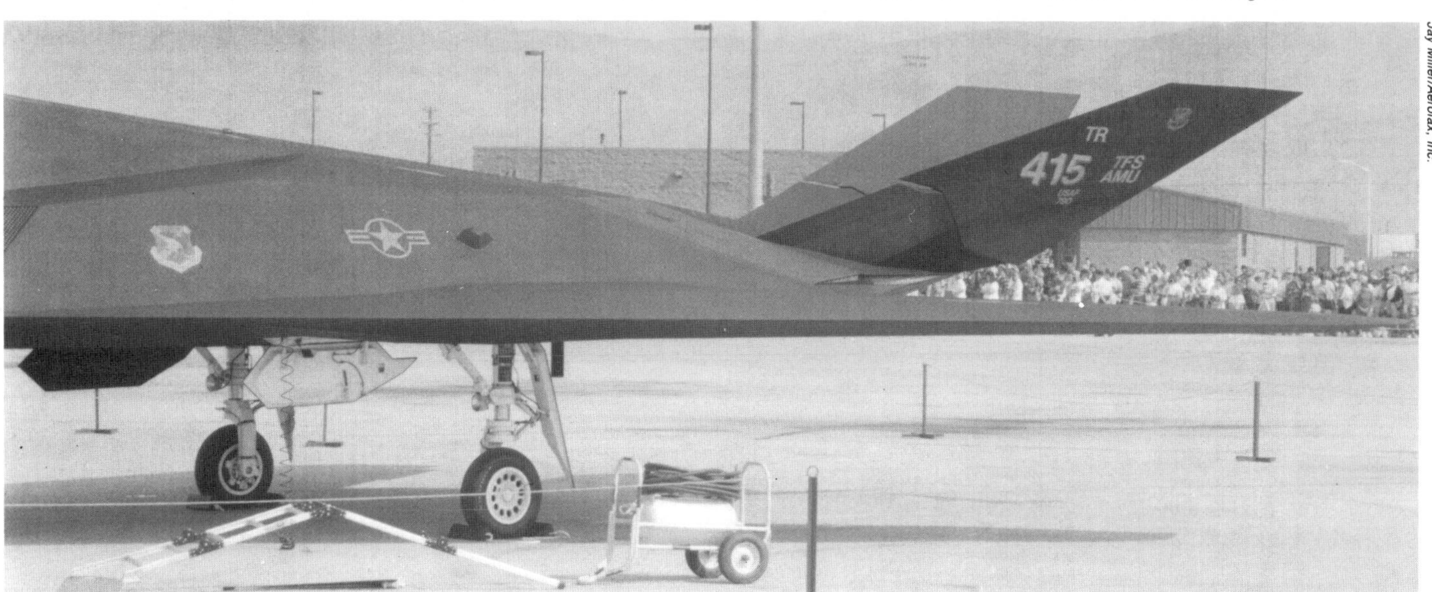

Jay Miller/Aerofax, Inc.

Aft section of aircraft and wing assembly present minimum cross-sectional area. Position of national insignia, unit badge, and radar reflector are readily discernible. Wing appears to have a thickness/chord ratio comparable to other contemporary attack aircraft such as the Vought A-7 "Corsair II".

Wingtip has interesting faceting arrangement which results in broadening taper to sharp edges. Where plates meet, however, there is some rounding of corners. Extreme tip, however, is very pointed. It is possible to mount a removable night-flying light on the wingtip if needed.

Jay Miller/Aerofax, Inc.

F-117A is equipped with both elevons (outboard) and flaperons. Both units are hydraulically boosted (thus the sag when the aircraft is powered-down). Faceting is carried through on inboard and outboard edges of these surfaces. Flaperons have three sealed hinge points, and elevons have four.

Jay Miller/Aerofax, Inc.

Wing leading edge is perfectly straight with no visible cap breaks. Slab surfaces meet at equally linear node lines. In cross section, wing has a hexagonal airfoil. Wings are wet with integral fuel tanks. All control surface and flap gaps are tightly sealed. Structure is primarily aluminum.

Jay Miller/Aerofax, Inc.

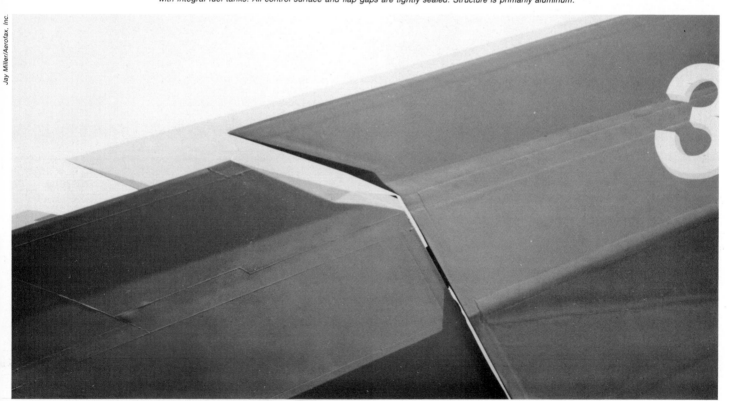

Detail view of RAM application to V-tail assembly. Vertical surfaces have unusual double-diamond airfoil section in consideration of RCS requirements. Actuation of all-moving portions is hydraulic. Moving surfaces are rudders and serve to input yaw moments only through F-16-type rudder pedals in cockpit.

Jay Miller/Aerofax, Inc.

V-tail is the first of the its kind on any operational manned combat aircraft in the U.S. Construction is presently aluminum with external RAM covering.

Jay Miller/Aerofax, Inc.

View looking forward between V-tail surfaces. Visible under extreme aft section of empennage are what appear to be viewing ports for aircraft RHAW system.

Jay Miller/Aerofax, Inc.

Nose landing gear is hydraulically steerable. Last three digits of aircraft serial number are in red.

Jay Miller/Aerofax, Inc.

Nose gear retracts forward and gear well door closes in concert. Door has separate hydraulic unit to ensure tight fit after closing. Nose gear is hydraulically steerable. Tire size is 22 x 6.6-10.

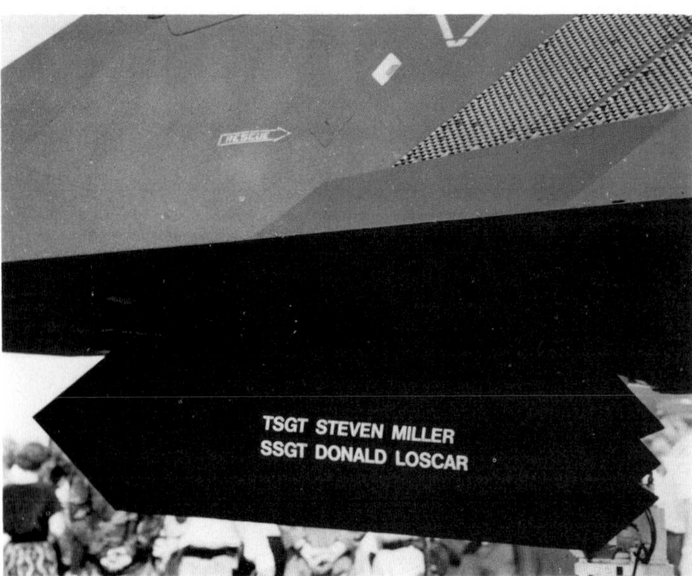

Jay Miller/Aerofax, Inc.

Nose gear door has serrated rear edge. Noteworthy is node line down door center. Visible on port side of door is access panel for external power and communication.

Jay Miller/Aerofax, Inc.

Main gear well forward door assembly is equipped with a shallow indentation to accommodate oversized wheel and tire. Bulge can be seen externally in the form of prism.

Jay Miller/Aerofax, Inc.

Jay Miller/Aerofax, Inc.

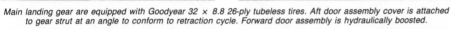

Main landing gear are equipped with Goodyear 32 × 8.8 26-ply tubeless tires. Aft door assembly cover is attached to gear strut at an angle to conform to retraction cycle. Forward door assembly is hydraulically boosted.

Jay Miller/Aerofax, Inc.

Main gear strut assembly is extremely rugged to accommodate heavy aircraft payloads.

Jay Miller/Aerofax, Inc.

Main landing gear retract forward via hydraulically-actuated scissor assembly. Right main gear well accommodates single-point refueling receptacle.

Jay Miller/Aerofax, Inc.

Original main gear brake assemblies were prone to fire following hot and heavy landings. Tube-like device on right is bolt-on radar reflector.

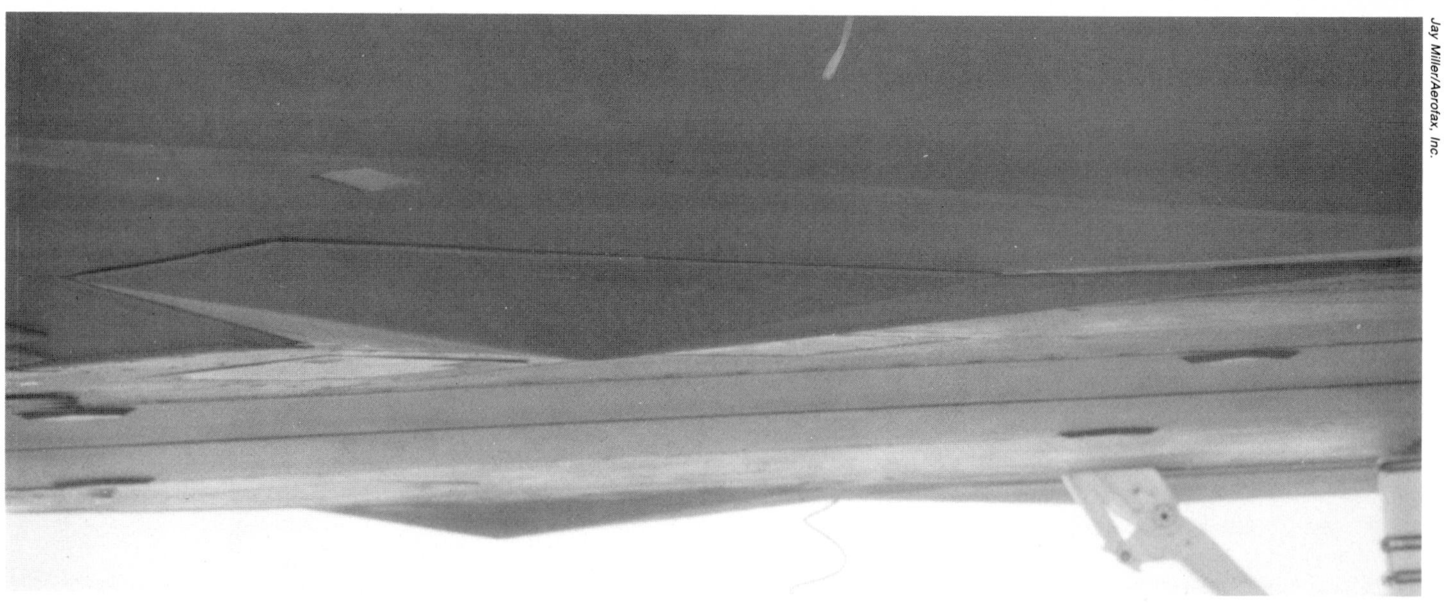

Jay Miller/Aerofax, Inc.

Forward section of gear well doors can be closed when the aircraft is on the ground. Their prism-like shape serves to cover bulge of oversized main gear wheel and tire assembly. Relatively tight fit is apparent. Main gear well door consists of two parts. Aft section is affixed to main gear strut.

Jay Miller/Aerofax, Inc.

Starboard intake screen. Screen is designed to reduce to negligible numbers the radar return normally generated by the engine compressor section face. Because of the screens, radar energy can only enter and return from directly in front of the aircraft. All other energy is dissipated long before it is reflected.

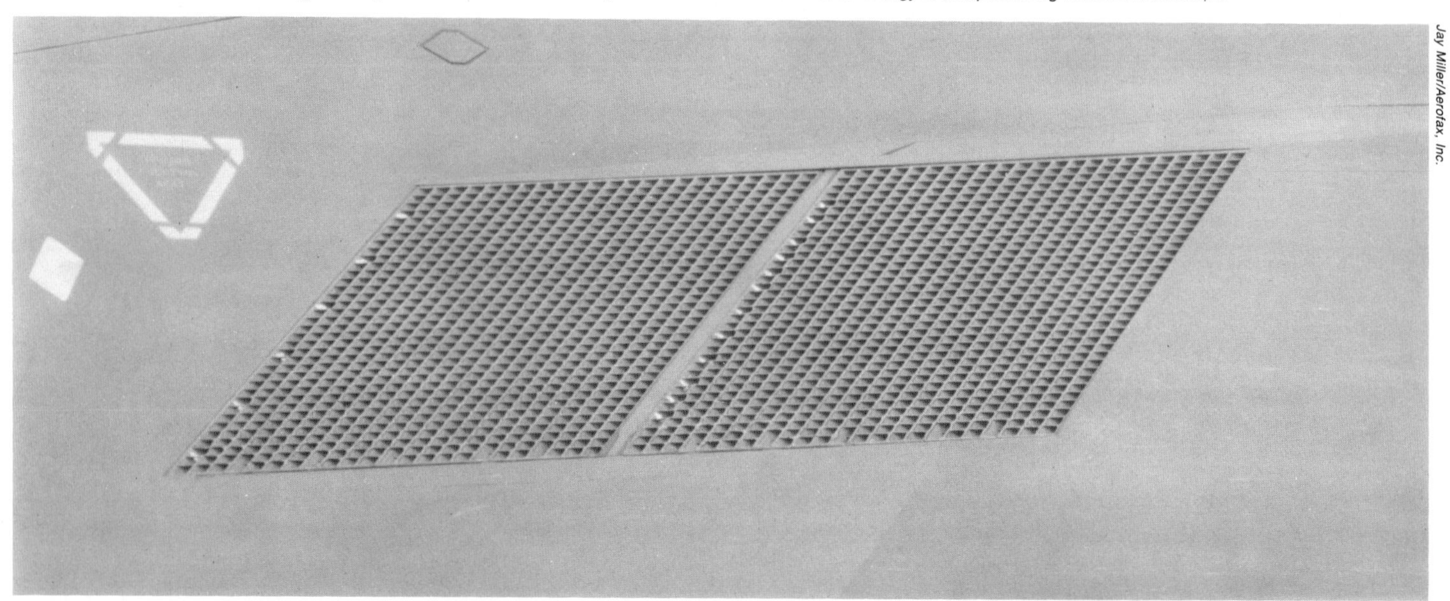

Jay Miller/Aerofax, Inc.

Port intake screen. Intake size is considerably larger than General Electric F404 requirements normally would dictate. This serves to compensate for the restricted intake flow caused by the screens. Ahead of and below screens is bypass intake slot for routing cooling air to exhaust plenum.

Jay Miller/Aerofax, Inc.

Jay Miller/Aerofax, Inc.

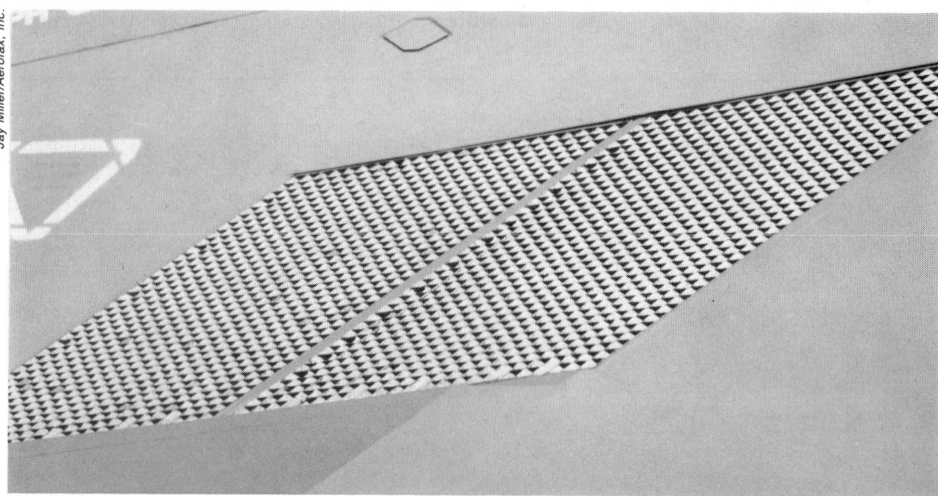

When viewed from almost head-on, intake screen is considerably less noticeable, underscoring its minimal effect on the intake airflow. Large duct area behind intake screens is conventional, without S-curves or related RCS-lowering gimmicks. Visible under wing leading edge is extended accessory attachment plug unit.

General Electric

General Electric

General Electric F404-GE-F1D2 turbofan engines utilized in the F-117A are quite similar to the McDonnell Douglas F/A-18's F404-GE-400 with the exception of the afterburner. The latter is deleted from the F-117A's engine and there are apparently dedicated modifications that enhance the engine's low-observable characteristics.

General Electric

General Electric F404-GE-F1D2 engines are representative of state-of-the-art low bypass turbofan technology. Visible are power take-off units with associated oil and hydraulic pump assemblies. Exhaust nozzle arrangement differs considerably from afterburner-equipped F404s.

Jay Miller/Aerofax, Inc.

Aft view of F-117A reveals how completely exhaust nozzles are shielded from low-attitude observation. Upswept empennage section considerably reduces exposure of hot exhaust nozzles to infrared sensors. Upper surface of lip is thoroughly insulated with "Space Shuttle"-type tiles to absorb heat.

Jay Miller/Aerofax, Inc.

Exhaust nozzles are flattened at the aft end of a large plenum into which the F404s eject their hot exhaust gases. Plenum serves as mixing point for cooler bypass air sucked in through slots just ahead of and beneath intakes. Coupled with ambient air mixed after passing over top of aircraft, the final exhaust efflux is relatively cool.

Jay Miller/Aerofax, Inc.

Flattened exhaust nozzles are divided into twelve exhaust slots. Gases exiting these impinge on the extended lower lip of the flattened empennage section which is covered with heat-absorbing "Shuttle"-like tiles. An ambient air mix cools the exhaust gases rapidly so that the infrared signature is minimized.

Jay Miller/Aerofax, Inc.

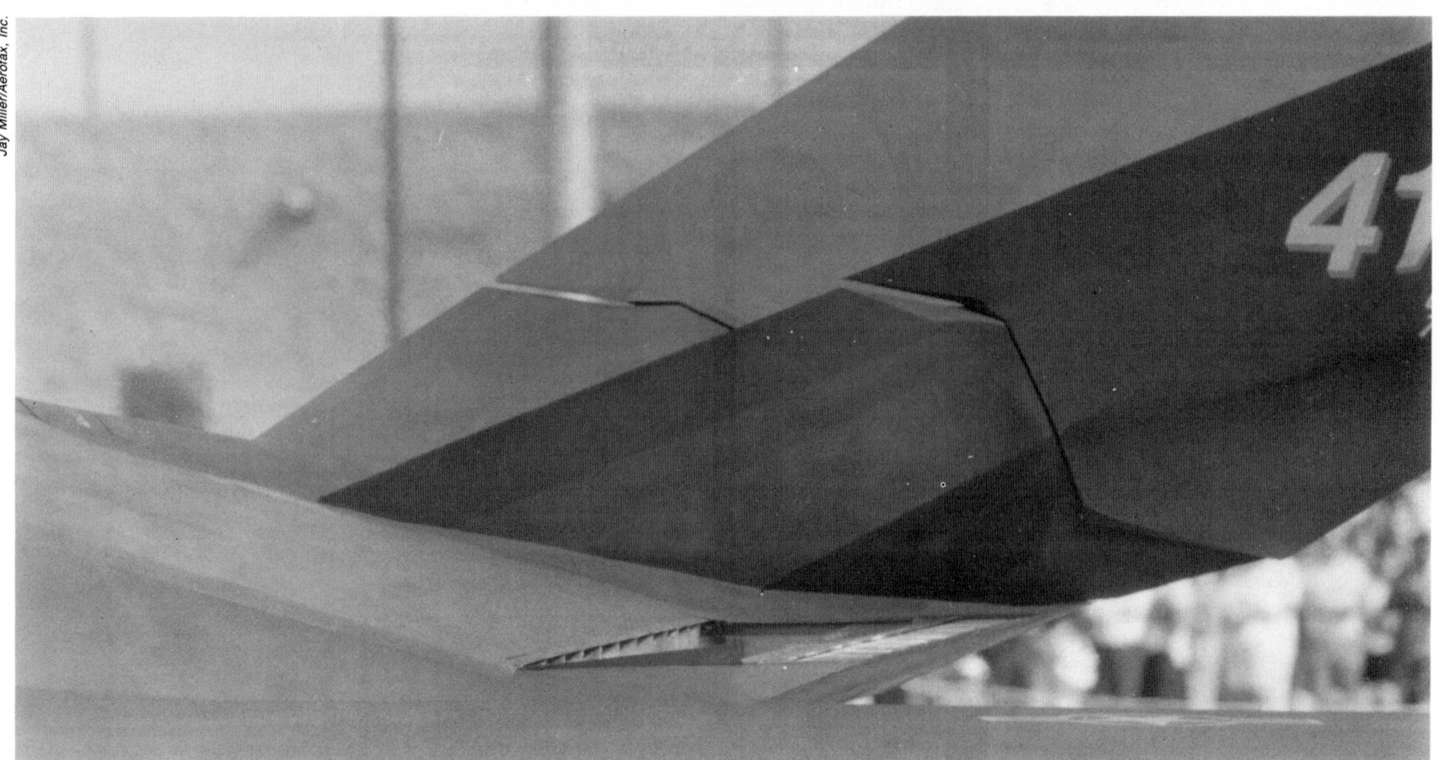

Flattened exhaust nozzles are only about six inches deep. In being recessed behind extended empennage lip, the infrared signature from anywhere beneath the aircraft is reduced to absolutely minimal values. Thrust degradation is minimized by providing greater cross-sectional area and minimizing obstructions in the plenum.

Jay Miller/Aerofax, Inc.

Upturned empennage trailing edge lip probably provides some aerodynamic input due to its shape. Though appearing rounded, it is, in fact, faceted like the rest of the aircraft. Ground level observation of the exhaust nozzles is restricted by the lip assembly as it stands over seven feet.

Jay Miller/Aerofax, Inc.

Bomb bay doors consist of two separate units which are hydraulically opened and closed. Hinge attachment points have multi-faceted covers. There appear to be two separate bays for weapons. Up to 5,000 lbs. of ordnance can be carried. Rectangular mark in foreground outlines tailhook enclosure.

Jay Miller/Aerofax, Inc.

Shoulder patch warn by the "Ghost Riders" of the 416th TFS of the 37th TFW. Patch depicts ghost-like apparition riding a pegasus-like horse and surrounded by stars.

Jay Miller/Aerofax, Inc.

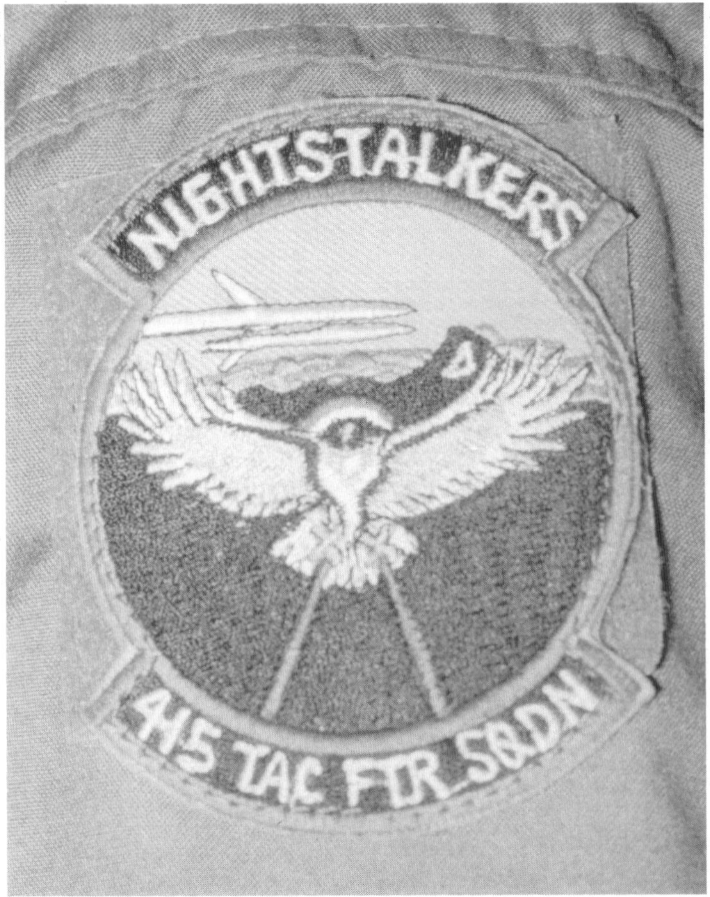

Shoulder patch warn by the "Nightstalkers" of the 415th TFS of the 37th TFW. Patch depicts hawk-like bird beaming destruction on targets below.